INTERMEDIATE LOAN

ENGLISH IN THE DIGITAL AGE

English in the Digital Age

Information and
Communications Technology (ICT)
and the Teaching of English

Edited by
Andrew Goodwyn

CASSELL
London and New York

Cassell

Wellington House
125 Strand
London WC2R 0BB

370 Lexington Avenue
New York
NY 10017–6550

First published 2000

British Library Cataloguing-in-Publication Data
A catalogue record for this book is available from the British Library.

ISBN   0-304-70623-X (paperback)

Typeset by Kenneth Burnley, Wirral, Cheshire.
Printed and bound in Great Britain by Creative Print and Design (Wales), Ebbw Vale.

Contents

The Contributors

Richard Andrews is Professor of Education at the Institute for Learning at the University of Hull, England, and is editor of a forthcoming series, the Cassell Guides to Educational Research.

Stephen Clarke is Senior Lecturer in the School of Education at the University of Leeds, England.

Jude Collins is Senior Lecturer in Education at the University of Ulster.

Andrew Goodwyn is Senior Lecturer in Education and Deputy Head of the School of Education at the University of Reading, England.

Leslie Hall is Assistant Professor of Educational Technology at the University of New Mexico, USA.

Les Lyons is Lecturer in Educational Technology and Media Education at La Trobe University, Bendigo, Australia.

Jane O'Donoghue is Key Stage 3 Co-ordinator at Heathfield Community College in East Sussex, England.

Penny Pence is Assistant Professor in the Division of Language, Literacy and Sociocultural Studies at the University of New Mexico, USA.

Vaughan Prain is Associate Professor in the School of Arts and Education at La Trobe University, Bendigo, Australia.

Don Zancanella is Associate Professor in the Division of Language, Literacy and Sociocultural Studies at the University of New Mexico, USA.

To

MARGARET GOODWYN,

a true, generous and indomitable spirit

and to

WINSTON BROOKES,

late convert to computers and colleague non-pareil

Introduction

This is a difficult time for all teachers, and for English teachers in particular. We are beset by insistent demands to teach our students the basics and to improve their literacy, and simultaneously to face up to a technological, computer-dominated future. Are these two sides of the same coin or are they irreconcilable demands, one looking to an imagined past, the other to an imagined future?

Readers will already know that reality involves a mixture of both. However, this is a very significant moment of change. This collection is aimed at helping the English-teaching community face up to a great challenge and to make progress in a principled and positive way. We already live in the age of information and communications technology, with almost every home, shop, business and street providing abundant evidence of our total reliance on the computer. The question 'Does the machine serve us or do we now serve the machine?' rightly concerns all educators. There have been endless absurd claims for technology, and we are right to be suspicious of them. The concept of computer 'literacy' is deeply flawed; many contributors to the collection show where claims for such literacy are vacuous or where they are of substance and of importance to teachers and students. At the same time this collection does celebrate the potential of technology to transform reading, writing, speaking and listening, and to help our students live successfully in a technological future. The collection pays close attention to where we are now and to what is possible now. It is full of very practical uses of the computer in English, shows how current teachers, student teachers and students are making exciting use of computers, and analyses the frequent frustrations and problems that beset us.

For readers in England and Wales the collection aims to provide material that helps to place into a comprehensible framework the relationship of ICT to schooling and to English in particular. In providing such a framework it examines recent history, conceptions of school 'English' and of literacy; it gives many examples both of currently available practical ideas and of the rich potential for the very immediate future. However, for all readers, regardless of geographical origin, it provides a broad view of what is happening in a range of different countries and settings. One key aspect of ICT is that it facilitates international and intra-national exchange at all levels. The contributors therefore reveal the nature of current, local activities and concerns, and connect these to the global networks to which we can all now belong.

My opening chapter attempts to be partly scene-setting and partly future-gazing. I am concerned to balance the inflated claims for 'computer literacy' with the genuine potential for new ways of learning and teaching. Computers will not replace English teachers, but they can certainly do some things better than any teacher; and they can, without doubt, improve the quality of our students' learning in English. I examine how teachers' attitudes and concepts are changing, how they are now accommodating ICT, and how this process is changing their view of what English both is and can become. Such a change involves a fundamental revision of the substance of English, viewing its nature more as a cultural resource than an inanimate heritage. I examine a series of teacher-initiated projects which reveal how much we can achieve now, and I look at some examples of reading and writing electronic text that offer tremendous potential for teachers and students in the next decade.

Richard Andrews' contribution acts as complement to my own chapter. Drawing on several years' experience of directing the national English and IT project in England, he reviews some key recent developments and offers excellent examples of current and emerging practice. He then develops a strong argument for English to become a more visualizing medium, a place where students' creative and artistic talents can be more fully and expressively developed.

In Jude Collins' very grounded study of what teachers in one part of the world are doing 'right now' and how they feel about the development of ICT in English, we have a glimpse of issues, concerns and possibilities. His chapter helps all teachers and researchers to appreciate the very real difficulties of the present and the opportunities of the future. It is also very helpful in giving us an insight into the challenge faced by student teachers; they will be living and teaching in an ICT world, but many schools they are learning to teach in now provide almost no scope for them to integrate ICT pedagogy into more traditional forms.

The view from Australia has more of a future orientation. Vaughan Prain and Les Lyons review some of the issues facing us all, especially the need to accept that literacy has genuinely changed and that teachers will have to find ways of helping their students to be critical users of ICT in English. Their two case studies provide interestingly different pictures. The first is similar to Jude Collins' picture of Northern Ireland, with teachers and students finding their way and reaching somewhat unsatisfactory outcomes. The second case shows us the confident and composed use of ICT as a means to research and to present new knowledge that is surely a view of the majority of classrooms in the not-too-distant future.

Jane O'Donoghue's chapter provides an excellent illustration of the exciting and challenging uses of ICT that exist within current resources and levels of teacher expertise. Her description of the numerous ways in which the Internet can support and extend English work show us that the Web really does live up to some of the exciting claims made for it. Her theme is essentially one of enhanced creativity, with opportunities for all pupils to contribute to this vast and dynamic resource. Her chapter is interlaced with comments from children, reminding us of how normal and ordinary it is for them to browse through the entire contents of this resource.

Children are also equally at home in the world of the electronic game. The serious and thoughtful review by Don Zancanella, Leslie Hall and Penny Pence of three computer games marks an important moment for English teachers. This North American contribution goes beyond any national boundaries. It confronts that secret fear that teachers have had for a long time, that some games actually are better than some books. Young people spend a long time playing these games because they are worth playing. The comparison with books is also shown to be intriguing but essentially misleading. Although the games that are analysed are narratives and include characters and settings, they are also experiences in a virtual world where every ending is inconclusive because one can always play again. A book (and the reader) may be different at each reading, but the ending is always the same. By being brave and taking the games seriously as a kind of literature, the authors have helped us to see the educative potential the games offer for classroom work. They challenge us to rethink our classroom boundaries and to explore the possibilities that such games provide just as much scope for a form of reader response as do some literary texts.

The potential for work with literature is explored throughout this book, but whatever else changes there seems to be no escape from the cult of Shakespeare. English teachers around the world seem to be increasingly skilled at teaching students about Shakespeare using a mixed media and drama approach. Stephen Clarke's chapter gives some inspirational ideas about how technology may offer us ways of working with our students that turn them into unlikely but willing textual scholars who, in interrogating the work of Shakespeare, discover both its value and its provisionality.

In considering how ICT may enhance and re-energize the study of Shakespeare, Stephen Clarke inevitably examines other 'technological' but more familiar resources such as video, film and audio tape. My final chapter is located in the virtual world of the text and in the potential of ICT to help us work with all media in critical and creative ways within the English classroom. It starts with a review of the capabilities of current word-processing software to provide far greater opportunities for us to do a whole range of textual work; we presently under-use the so-called 'basic' functions available with almost any package. We also under-use on the computer textual activities familiar in classrooms, such as cloze and sequencing, and I try to show how much more productive these can be if used by thoughtful English teachers. In examining these activities I try to demonstrate how ICT brings together in productive ways various modes that hitherto have been treated as distinct. The most obvious conflation is reading and writing, as the reader of an electronic text can become its re-writer, its critic and its mentor. Speaking and writing blur in e-mail. Reading and listening blur as the text is read to us and illustrated at the same time. Overall the chapter concludes the book with a celebration of some of the potential for ICT to make the English classroom the most exciting place for students and teachers to work together.

ANDREW GOODWYN
April 1999

Chapter 1

'A Bringer of New Things':
An English Teacher in the Computer Age?

ANDREW GOODWYN

> We are moving away from literature book-based culture, it's a shift in youth. It's a general move, towards television, video, computer games in their own life – out of school you're fighting a society that is moving away from literature towards a leisure-based, easier culture and the reading and literature themes look too hard – we are between the generations, sort of juggling reading and writing alongside IT.
>
> (an English teacher quoted in Goodwyn *et al.*, 1997)

> And slowly answer'd Arthur from the barge:
> 'The old order changeth, yielding place to new',
> And God fulfils himself in many ways,
> Lest one good custom should corrupt the world.
>
> (Tennyson, 'The Idylls of the King',
> *The Passing of Arthur*, 1.407)

The teacher's comment, 'we are between the generations', exactly captures the dilemma for many educators at the beginning of the twenty-first century. They are in between the print/literature generation and the new generations concerned, they feel, with electronic media of all kinds. There is also a sense of alienation from young people who seem to be opting for this 'easier, leisure culture', the implication being that our hard-won knowledge base is to be neglected and even lost. Where are the future custodians to come from? For teachers of literature this dramatizes a fear that books will lose their current high status, and so therefore will the teachers of literature.

Tennyson's lines, written in the midst of the Industrial Revolution in the 1860s, remind us that much of literature is not just profoundly concerned with the 'human condition' but with our eternally mixed feelings about stability and change. We may presently, as the teacher above does, feel an unease and an anxiety about the specific nature of technological change but it is important to note that, paradoxically, anxiety is our normal reaction and that we, collectively, have faced such challenges in every century and must face them in perpetuum. I. A. Richards, early in the twentieth century, pointed out that a 'book is a machine to think with' (Richards, 1924, p. 1); in other words that literature is itself a technology, a way of accomplishing something for writers and readers.

Tennyson's life as an artist also has a dimension that is of value to us at the end of the twentieth century, and his use of the Arthurian myth sheds light on our current concerns. He wrote at a time of powerful national self-consciousness, when the 'British' nation was considering its empire building and industrial and technological future; I am aware that for many readers there never has been any such nation. He also became the Poet Laureate, eventually a Lord, and was given a representative status of his nation that he sought to fulfil. Approaching the end of the nineteenth century raised issues about a national future in a new, dynamic and unpredictable age. It was a time of unprecedented rapid change and industrialization. It was, as now, a time of great human crisis. The nature of people's work and their 'value' as human beings were uncertain and seemed unpredictable. While many lived in squalor and poverty, others amassed vast fortunes. The 'modern' urbanized city was emerging as the way we would have to live from then on. Parallels and remarkable differences abound between the late Victorian age and the beginnings of the global computer age. Across the then English-speaking world artists of all kinds struggled to make sense of this new and dubious form of civilization.

Tennyson, like many other artists, partly looked back, as do many people now, to the past for a source of both stability and inspiration. He selected the great Arthurian myth as a unifying and morally uplifting centre for a nation challenged by change and social upheaval. He was interested in science and change, even fascinated by its potential, and so indicative references are constantly found throughout his work. His Arthur reflects on the necessity and desirability of change as his old order passes on. Once we have an order then the innovative must challenge and eventually change it. However, Tennyson is also a useful point of reference because late in life he accepted a role as national spokesman; this clearly hampered and hindered his authenticity as an individual voice. When we study Tennyson we can trace these tensions and compromises in his later work: he is not just significant as a poet, but as a signifier of a national ideology. ICT, as I hope I will show in my concluding chapter in the collection, enables us to explore the significant and the signifying in powerful new ways. It is also not accidental that my use of Tennyson's 'Ulysses' poem comes from his early, uncompromised period.

For teachers of English these are particularly confusing and difficult times: teachers fall between the old and new orders, their students already seem more than comfortable in the New Age, aliens in the classroom (Kress, 1997). An age of technology that seems to threaten many stabilities also serves to remind us that literature is a great source of wisdom, not solely about the past but equally about the future. Through the iconic figure of the dying Arthur, Tennyson reflects on the inevitability and desirability of change. Every generation must be 'in between' and the old order not only has to change but it must also 'give way'.

Schools in the developed world are at a point of significant change, the sense of being 'in between' is stronger than usual, and we must all recognize the authenticity of such tensions. I am not arguing, simplistically or naïvely, that computers in themselves are a good thing. Teachers have very good reasons for questioning the intrinsic value of computers and related technologies. Several recent studies have attempted to analyse the advent of 'computer literacy' and to critique its claims and its espoused purpose (for a summary see Goodson and Mangan, 1996). These studies have raised some of the following concerns. First, what is 'computer literacy', what on earth does such a phrase mean? Second, there seems to be little active questioning of its value; everyone simply and perhaps simplistically seems to view the future as computer-dominated, therefore schools must acquire as much hardware as possible and ensure that all their pupils leave school computer literate. In their promotional literature, schools now lay great stress on their technological capabilities and parents take note of this. A useful corrective might be that the developed world is also car-dominated but we do not spend energy in school ensuring that students can drive, i.e. are car-literate, before they leave. However, this analogy has a clear weakness which I will explore below. The key fourth point, which follows on from this, is that teachers in general have yet to be persuaded of the educational validity of many of the transformative and empowering claims made for computer literacy. The danger seems to be that their critical concerns will simply be ignored and they will be treated as antiquated luddites as opposed to being respected as critical professionals. This chapter and this book will treat readers as the latter, and although the writers collectively hold positive views of what computers can do for our students' learning, you will still find plenty of cautionary notes. Throughout, there is a clear emphasis on the role of the teacher in using the technology as a means to an educative end, never as an end in itself.

The advent of technology also brings specific problems that we will have to face. For example, certain books are called 'corrupt' and certainly influence minds, but a single corrupt computer disc can cause immense damage to people's lives and livelihoods. The age of the network brings the phenomenon of the virus, recent ones having been so powerful as to cause inestimable financial damage. The Internet may soon replace television as the perceived enemy of all things good, providing access to pornography, fascist and racist organizations and to websites that help children to design bombs and weapons. Computer games and simulations seem to be extremely addictive to children and adults alike. The working practices of many adults, hunched over a screen for a long working day, ignoring all health and safety guidance, suggest a different form of work-related addiction. Now that the computer at home is linked to the one at work and the portable allows one to 'plug in' almost anywhere in the world, one need never be out of touch with work, even if that was the purpose of 'getting away'.

These cautions and concerns must receive appropriate and sustained attention. It is also important to avoid the inflated rhetoric of the first 'schools and computers' phase, discussed below. However, it is equally valid to examine current benefits to be found from using ICT in the English classroom and to speculate on the positive potential we are just beginning to understand.

THE GLEAMS OF AN UNTRAVELLED WORLD

> I am a part of all that I have met;
> Yet all experience is an arch wherethrough
> Gleams that untravelled world, whose margin fades
> For ever and for ever when I move.
>
> (Tennyson, 'Ulysses', 1834)

Tennyson's lines might have been written today: for a child facing a computer screen about to embark on a voyage across the Internet, the screen can be an arch of truly awesome significance. Tennyson's Ulysses refuses to rest. He chooses 'To follow knowledge like a sinking star/Beyond the utmost bound of human thought'; he determines to remain 'A bringer of new things'. That strikes me as a wonderful motto for English teachers, tempted perhaps by the safe harbour of literature but for whom a 'newer world' offers new possibilities.

This opening chapter attempts to help teachers and other educators position themselves in an informed and principled way in what otherwise may seem like a welter of threats and instabilities. I shall begin by reviewing why there is a fundamental conceptual issue for all teachers of language and literature to come to terms with in their own specific way. In order to make sense of this I shall look back at some earlier issues surrounding computer use in English, and consider where we can say real progress has been made, although such progress is visible in isolated examples rather than in general 'good practice'.

I shall examine some of these examples for their significance for us now as we grapple, as a professional community, with how our practices move from 'the old order' to 'the new'. I shall then consider a key issue for English teachers about what our curriculum will need to look like as we enter a transitional period in which the multi-faceted electronic text becomes the typical textual form, and the printed text will begin to enjoy a different status. Although I shall draw almost exclusively on my UK experience I think it clear from the chapters that follow, which draw from other English-speaking environments, that we are all in the same Homeric boat. For every teacher there is the question of turning ideas into a practical reality. This chapter will move towards a clear consideration of that reality but if, like Ulysses, we 'are to seek a newer world', then we must understand why we are leaving the old one. At this point it is worth noting that many of our students have already arrived and are themselves keen to help us arrive safely. This is a positive development, not a problem.

INHERITING YOUR CULTURE?

> Though much is taken, much abides. (Tennyson, *ibid.*)

Much of my interest over the last decade has been located in English teachers' thinking. The question I constantly ask them is 'What do you mean by English? What is this subject and what is it for?' One reason for the urgency of this question has been because, in most English-speaking countries around the world, there is an explicit attempt by people, usually government 'agencies' of one kind or another, to insist on a version of English that they feel the community is entitled to receive. This is not the first time that prescriptions have been placed on English teachers around the globe from local to national level, but there is a coherence about the prescriptions themselves and a disempowering of teachers which is decidedly on a grander and more oppressive scale. As several UK English teachers recently expressed it:

> Excellent and inspirational teachers of English do not work best in a cage. A love of English is the last thing you need to teach to these orders and syllabuses.
>
> As usual we are trying hard to find ways around the problem rather than shouting loudly that it is inappropriate, alienating students from the subject culturally and intellectually. Goodness knows what we would do without decent films of these texts.
>
> Literature in the NC supports bias – white, middle class, Anglo Saxon Christian male attitudes. Time for change. More realistic guidelines rooted in late twentieth-century and real experience rather than halcyon days that never really existed. I feel remarkably angry about recent developments in English.
>
> What I have resented in recent years, more than anything, is the erosion of my professional judgement. We have always taught Shakespeare and pre-twentieth-century literature but I strongly object to not being able to decide for myself when to introduce my students to them (and which texts to use). We are also inexorably being forced to teach to the paltry tests. (By the way, why was Model 6 left out? English Which Can Be Reduced To Testing?) The level of prescription now is ludicrous. Teachers teach best when they are enthused about a text/topic they are teaching. When these are imposed and wheeled out year after year it becomes more and more difficult to maintain one's freshness and enthusiasm. (Goodwyn and Findlay, 1999)

The relevance of this issue for my chapter is that as teachers either embrace computer technology willingly or grudgingly (something I discuss below) they discover that a great deal of power comes back to them. Government agencies – essentially preservative, controlling bodies – have little idea of how their current power will be eroded by the destabilizing effects of the textual fluidity and creative anarchy of the World Wide Web – even the humblest word processor gives the writer enormous creative power. However, I shall rein back the evangelism (for now) and seek to clarify my argument.

The 'developed' nations of the world have established systematic forms of education, creating largely literate and numerate populations; they have each grappled with the difficult, essentially unanswerable question: 'What culture or cultures should this systematic education provide?' In other words a 'universal' education immediately problematizes 'culture'; the longer the history of that educational system and the greater its attempt to provide more and more education, the tougher the problem becomes. There is then a kind of inevitable logic to government agencies insisting that, as no one else, least of all cultured people, can define culture, they will.

This assertion of a predominantly national culture foregrounds the past. What shall the nation pass on to the next generation? Essentially the nation has to 'make its will' to ensure that the next generation shall inherit what it rightfully should. Inevitably this taking stock of the nation's cultural resources leads to the next generation being bequeathed some wonderful things, and some worn-out old bits and pieces that have sentimental value and leave the inheritors guiltily putting them in the attic.

Culture, however, is always 'happening', hence every generation experiences it and redefines it. English teachers are in the thick of this experience, at once charged, like cultural accountants, with executing the nation's will, distributing the inheritance and, as cultured people, with experiencing a living culture as it happens. This living culture is now the culture of the computer, the Internet, the global media, the hypertext, the interactive encyclopaedia and, of course, the book. It is also an intra-national culture: that is, one that both reveals other cultures to each other and simultaneously challenges each culture, making conservative elements feel superior and hostile while making innovative elements feel equal and excited. A striking example of this tendency is television programmes about the television programmes of other cultures, where a presenter helps the audience to see how foolish and alien these 'foreign' programmes can be.

To return to teachers, I think English teachers, certainly in the National Curriculum structure of England, have increasingly rejected the role of cultural accountant. Research (Goodwyn and Findlay, 1999) shows that the nationalistic Cultural Heritage model enshrined increasingly in the prescriptive curriculum is rejected by English teachers. Under this pressure they have increasingly espoused their fundamental pedagogical model, Personal Growth: a child-centred model, positioning students as participants in, and creators of, culture as opposed to merely inheritors of someone else's. At the same time, these teachers clearly recognize that young people live in a media-dominated world, and with a mixture of protective and empowering motives they want their students to both enjoy and evaluate the media world.

So an interest in a cultural analysis stance continues to grow and becomes a powerful element in English teachers' thinking. In order to think clearly about how to make the most of ICT in English and also how to resist some of the narrow, functionalist tendencies in computer literacy, we need to look further back before stepping forward.

MEDIA EDUCATION AND INFORMATION TECHNOLOGY SHARE A CHAPTER

Some work of noble note may yet be done. (Tennyson, *ibid.*)

In 1989 the National Curriculum for English was created by the Cox Committee, a committee appointed by a government agency. The curriculum they designed does indeed now look like a 'work of noble note'; it certainly defined culture as a living, multi-faceted, exciting part of life, that work has its own story (Cox, 1991). The key point for our purposes in coming to understand where technology will invigorate English is that the Cox Report (DES, 1989) put Media Education and Information Technology in one short but significant chapter. It is clear that they did this partly innocently, not knowing quite what to do with these new and somewhat awkward elements, yet keenly aware that they would shape the future. I would argue that those two areas are now becoming one, something signalled in the emergence of the term Information and Communications Technology. I shall look at the practical effects of this in my later chapter (Chapter 8).

If the Cox Report was unknowingly prophetic, the reality of the late 1980s and early 1990s gave very little evidence of that prophecy's validity. The first National Curriculum was to a large extent welcomed by English teachers, but the constant revisions and interferences by government agencies has since produced a high degree of negativity. This hostility has confused many issues, one such being the role of then IT (now ICT) in English. However, this book will provide plenty of evidence for the fundamental place of ICT in English, both in its current shape and in its twenty-first-century form.

Recent research (Goodwyn and Findlay, 1999) shows very clearly that English teachers are redefining their subject, recognizing the tensions between a moribund cultural heritage model and their focus on a growth model of children joining, sharing and participating in culture. Such redefinitions are difficult and confusing. Certainly in the time from 1989 to 1999 English teachers have now given equal place, if not status, to media education work. I would argue that a more cultural analysis view of all texts is emerging and that this will be a very timely reconceptualization enabling the community to make the most of computers and to resist computers constraining them.

In order to illustrate this point I shall refer in summary form to one piece of research (Goodwyn *et al.*, 1997). This was an investigation into the views of English teachers about the place of ICT in English, especially in relation to school students' literacy. The quotation that heads this chapter comes from that research. Having interviewed both teachers and student teachers in different parts of England we identified the following categories of teachers defined by their attitudes towards ICT in English. Those in the 'fearful' category (about one-fifth) found computers bewildering, threatening and saw them as alienating and anti-social. They felt attached to a very different past, 'I just cannot get away from pen and paper'; another said 'Books have to be central, something you can open and read at any point.' For these teachers computers represent an 'other', an 'opposition'. For some teachers, feelings are much more mixed and a third of teachers in the study were unsure about the future; they are the 'unresolved'. For them ICT offers considerable potential for their students but they tend to see it as a motivator, especially valuable for the less-able but with dangers attached; perhaps children may lose their social skills. However, just over half the teachers were clearly now 'optimists' and these were teachers of all kinds of ages and degrees of experience. They felt that ICT was empowering and stimulating, providing genuinely new forms of communication and means of gaining information and access to texts of all kinds, that it broadens the whole concept of literacy, giving children and adults masses of opportunity to be active learners and meaning-makers. However, they had no illusions about magic solutions; they identified many problems associated with access to equipment, training for teachers and the oversimplistic view of computers held by some who saw them as replacing teachers.

I am arguing that the community is in the process of redefining its purpose and that the external pressure of prescription and the internal pressure of child-centredness are producing a powerful new rationale for the subject, one that makes computer technology an enhancing element. The subsequent chapters in the book are full of instances of what that enhancement can do now and of its potential for our future. The concerns outlined above about computer literacy are important points and a useful corrective to bear in mind. However, the objections of the 'fearful' and the 'unresolved' are based on little real experience and on no considered evidence. It would be wrong simply to dismiss these fears, but it is just as important to put them into perspective. One key perspective is that other teachers have managed to make exciting and powerful use of ICT in English and they do have real experience and evidence of its value. I am going to draw here on some current instances of such innovative practice so that when I move on to consider what a new English curriculum may look like I can show where that view connects with current realities.

> How dull it is to pause, to make an end,
> To rust unburnished, not to shine in use!
> (Tennyson, *ibid.*, 1.22–23)

It is important to recognize that we are facing up to the new technologies for a second time. There was a false dawn in the mid- to late-1980s; this was the period in which the very first generation of computers came into schools. In the UK this was the age of the BBC computer and the Amstrad PCW. A small group of teachers instantly felt the possibilities of the new technologies and an early book such as Phil Moore's *Using Computers in English* (Moore, 1986) shows how clearly that potential was seen. However, there was a powerful and very negative reaction to the vastly inflated claims of this period. Hardware and software in schools was meagre in supply and poor in quality, as it was in the home. The computer was by no means common at work except in certain key areas such as the military and in research.

In fact, this early period served mainly to confirm the majority of teachers in their opposition to the computer age. Their experience (see Goodwyn *et al.*, 1997) was confined to attending one or two days of training, just enough to interest but confuse them and to return them to work environments where there was no opportunity to follow up and use these fragile skills. The key changes have not been in schools but they have been in the work and domestic environments where the computer has become a normal, ordinary and integrated element. Most schools have been left far behind and teachers constantly lament their incompetence.

However, it is important to stress that many teachers in the UK have found imaginative ways to move forward, incorporating ICT into their normal work during the 1990s. This progress is even more impressive because there has been no real support and no leadership or direction, with the exception of support from the former NCET and the English and IT project cited below (Goodwyn, 1997b, 1998). Current governmental initiatives throughout the developed world reflect this recognition that schools and teachers have long been neglected and that real investment is now essential. However, much has been done that can encourage us, that has not been reliant on substantial investment.

A simple but profound example comes from the initial CD-Roms project in England and Wales. This initiative simply provided some primary schools with at least one, and sometimes two, computers that had CD drives and with several current 'educational' CD-Roms. The teachers were asked to experiment with their use and to evaluate their impact on their children's learning. Teachers were soon dissatisfied with children's initial 'reading' of information texts. Some of the early reference works were simply versions of the print text, an encyclopaedia for example, and the texts were verbose and complex. Children searching for information tended to download and then simplistically paste the text without really understanding it. The teachers soon encouraged their classes to begin by cutting out the text they wanted and then to rewrite it for their own age group, simplifying text and/or explaining difficult words and concepts. This transforms the activity into a dynamic interaction between a reading-oriented text and a writer-oriented text with pupils transforming this given text into their own work, drawing on the existing textual information and structures as a scaffold; this intervention into a given text is discussed at length in my final chapter.

Another primary example focused on trying to make use of existing computers to improve children's writing and their consciousness of being a writer. This project involved placing pupils in pairs – one older pupil and one less experienced writer – to write fairy stories. The older pupil's role was to help the younger write a story of his or her own. This interaction took place on a regular basis over a series of weeks so that the story gradually developed and built up. The two wrote and revised on screen in large print, with the story being printed out from time to time in order to see the whole text. The older pupils therefore acted as writing mentor and adviser, performing a secretarial and developmental function. The younger writers were able to see their words and ideas on the page beyond their current scope to write. The result was a collaborative text but one owned by the younger writer; the older writer was also inducted into the process of writing in a very conscious way. There may well be long-term benefits of such an approach, but research needs to be done to establish and evaluate the results. Teachers involved in the project were convinced that it had real value.

A final example comes from a tiny 40-pupil school in a very rural area. It is tempting to think in the age of television and radio that all children everywhere are 'in touch' with the world. However, remoteness can exist in very traditional ways. '. . . we are such an isolated little school' as the head commented, and so the staff had decided to risk investing in one up-to-date computer. The school at once involved all its pupils in the creation of a school website, and the use of e-mail. As the head put it: 'One boy last year hadn't even been out of the village and yet there he was corresponding with people from all over the world. I think it has given them amazing confidence. We now have visitors from all over the world dropping into the school and the children are so at ease with them.' Having visited the school myself I can attest to this confidence and openness in the children, who clearly felt in touch in a very positive way with the wider world. It is also worth sounding a cautionary note here. Making the world accessible to children carries the danger of making them accessible to the world. What might be categorized as an inevitably naïve stance towards the Internet in its early days needs now to be replaced with a more 'knowing' and guarded attitude.

An exciting example that spans the primary and secondary sectors shows how a simple idea can become a powerful, potentially long-term learning resource for a community. In this project a teacher had the vision to see the enormous potential of the CD-Rom as a writing tool, to create a textual database of children's work. The basic concept was to capture the writing of children from ages 5 to 16, following individuals from their earliest writings in primary school through to their closing statements before they left school and entered the adult world. Once a CD writer became affordable in the mid-1990s it became possible to create such a database. This database can have a number of functions. In imitation of the ancient world it can act as a repository and archive of writing, a library of representative written texts. Such an archive also serves as a resource for students and teachers, providing hundreds of examples and models of texts. More in the spirit of the age of electronic text it can also be constantly written to and revised; it is therefore a never-finished, always-developing, dynamic field of writing that each student can add to. As an electronic archive it can also be searched very rapidly and sections retrieved by a teacher or a student; this reveals a profound difference between such a database and a filing cabinet full of children's writing. Such a physical archive is inevitably organized in one physical way and every text is static and fixed. Electronic texts can always be regrouped and rewritten, they are a dynamic resource. Such a database can also be easily and rapidly exchanged with other writing communities, potentially around the globe; something that is not likely to happen with a filing cabinet full of old papers.

AN INNOVATIVE RATHER THAN A PRESERVATIVE CURRICULUM

One inevitable result of the current preservative attitude to the English curriculum is that some have tried to imagine and formulate a new, innovative curriculum. Such views (Kress, 1997; Tweddle *et al.*, 1997; Goodwyn, 1998) have helped to inform the thinking in this section but here we will focus on the curriculum in relation principally to ICT. Any major new element in an established curriculum competes for space and challenges teachers' expertise and confidence. Some teachers seize on such innovative areas as a refreshing and stimulating opportunity, while others find it a threat and a destabilizing concern. For example, when media education began to influence English teaching in the late 1980s one result was a proliferation of classroom tasks that involved students in producing newspaper accounts; this was in addition to the English teachers' traditional concern with advertising. Sometimes these newspaper accounts were journalistic versions of literary events, for example, reports in the *Verona Times* of the riot at the beginning of *Romeo and Juliet*, or articles about topical issues. In themselves these were challenging and appropriate writing tasks but they usually ignored two key points. The first was media context: these articles were somehow neutral, written for any newspaper, they just demonstrated an understanding of the original text and of newspapers (Goodwyn, 1992). The second was to do with development: teachers were not in a position to think about how writing a newspaper article in senior school should build on work completed in the junior part of the school; it tended to be more of the same with improvement implied by repetition.

There is a strong parallel with the above stage of integrating Media Education into English and the use of computer technology in most current English curricula in schools. These two issues, i.e. contextualizing student activities within the actual technological capability of computers and merely repeating as opposed to creating an incremental and developmental use of them, similarly affect current practice with the use of ICT in English. This is certainly not the fault of good teachers of English but it is something that they will soon have to deal with. ICT work in English is not neutral; just using ICT is of little value. The research cited above demonstrates that for some teachers the actual use of ICT is the intrinsic motivating purpose because it captures the interest and enthusiasm of students. There is some support for this idea but in the computer/media age this motivational force will be relatively short-lived. ICT is only valuable when it is providing intrinsic benefits. The next section examines some of the key benefits of ICT and provides some practical illustration of their value.

However, it also puts forward a view of English in which its curriculum balances past, present and future. Its argument is that the past is essentially a cultural resource for all of us; it is only a heritage insofar as you or I make it one because there is no monolithic or monocultural heritage, only claims – often very interesting and well-thought-out claims – for what it ought to be. Certainly the idea of what an English heritage is claimed to be is something that all our students should investigate, especially if they can compare it with the claims made for an American, Australian or European heritage. Culture exists in the present and is being created all around us, so English is one forum in which it is experienced and created. All our students look forward, appropriately naïvely, to 'making it' in the future. The English curriculum is a place for enjoying and reflecting on our cultural resources, debating their values, and imagining and designing our futures. In English there is a specific and crucial emphasis on language and ICT offers us powerful new ways of working with language and other symbolic systems (see my final chapter).

One key aspect of the electronic media is that they foreground provisionality, that is the concept that a text is infinitely changeable, just as it is in the mind of its creator. There may well be a 'final' version in the sense that one writer/reader stops working on that text, but that version is never a final one to any other writer/reader, even when this text has assumed a highly significant status. Before examining this concept within the classroom context it is important to note that this recognition is a part of a larger intellectual recognition.

There is a remarkable convergence between recent thinking in the fields that might loosely be defined as literary theory, reader response theory and more general theories of knowledge. I shall sum this up very simply in order to move to the key issue for teachers of how it opens up new potential in English teaching. Literary criticism/theory has become a highly fragmented field: it is now infinitely specialized and has abandoned the universal project. Critics do not sum up the achievements of a particular text; they take a position, recognizing that many others are possible. The educational field of reader-response argues for a view of students as readers, discovering interpretations that are themselves always to be revised by a combination of greater insights created by dialogue about texts, and developed through an increasing knowledge of texts and the readers' own incremental life experience. Technology has been one element in a general review of how we acquire and retain knowledge. At the risk of a vast generalization, the creation of electronic information has helped us to see that individuals are active agents in generating what is their own knowledge, and that such knowledge can exist in shared forms but the forms themselves are provisional. For example, the act of reading is itself an active creation of the text's meanings, but the electronic text can simultaneously be rewritten. I am not suggesting that readers will become obsessed with 'interfering' with every text but I am certain that readers will generally feel in more control of the text and feel less controlled by it. For teachers this raises a number of possibilities, and the first implication of provisionality concerns 'composing'.

RE-COMPOSING TEXTS?

The creation of any meaningful text is hard work. One is not sure what one means until one has tried to mean it. Often a first reaction is to know that one has expressed a meaning but it is not yet what one means to say. The process of writing is always alerting us to the potential we have to make meaning and reminding us of its precarious nature. A piece of paper is a very useful space for composing, for jotting down words, numbers, symbols, representational images and so on. Several pieces of paper allow one to spread out, fill the table/desk and yet keep all these bits within vision. One's concentrated attention can only be on a small space at a time but the 'bigger' picture is to some extent available. The composition of a text on a screen has similarities but there is at least one key difference as an act of composition, its provisional nature. This can be illustrated by two examples that show the potential for English teachers.

Of all activities that dominate English teachers' time none is so relentless as 'marking', the physical act of putting marks on students' work. No one doubts the importance of such attention to each student but most teachers frequently doubt that their efforts are making the difference that they hope to achieve. Currently an individual student writes the text and a teacher marks and/or grades it. The student may then correct that text and may respond to the teacher's comments and suggestions. However, the physical nature of such texts means that a record of that teacher/student interchange is preserved, but little else. If the student completes a truly provisional, electronic text, then the teacher has far more options.

One simple and vital difference is that the student can expect a composition to be revisited and revised a number of times – and not necessarily immediately. Many writers need a little distance from their original text before they are able to 'go at it' again. This is partly because writing is physically, mentally and often emotionally wearing. It is also because one writes 'in' one's text, struggling to complete it. The written English language is chiefly structured in a linear way, with word and paragraph order requiring a relentless move from beginning to end. However, our minds are most definitely capable of very different modes of creative and analytical sequencing. When we are confident enough as writers to 'get down' our first draft then at that stage we 'are' that first draft, that is the 'position' we have stopped at. We may immediately see minor errors and infelicities. However, for many writers there is a very positive need to walk away from the text and to return to it at a later stage.

Currently there is always severe pressure on students to produce a final version so that the teacher can assess it. Some pressure is helpful and motivating. There is often an argument that students must learn to cope with pressure on their writing as they will face tests in school and they will face deadlines in adult life. Like all common-sense clichés this has an element of truth. However, teachers, especially English teachers, are quite able to distinguish between the extrinsic motivation, which has its place, and the intrinsic motivation that comes from a writer having something to say and also the conviction that 'saying it the right way' will take time and effort. A great deal of writing under pressure is forced, inaccurate and inadequate. In the educational attempt to balance such pressure, teachers will find that technology gives them far greater flexibility, so they can make the most of this potential in the way they support and monitor a student's development as a writer. For example, students might also be able to offer their teacher, their critical friend, more than one version of, say, a poem and invite the teacher to produce a version or versions. Equally with texts such as the essay, the attempt to create an argument, teachers and students have far more opportunity to 'play with' the logic and emotional structures of their compositions, with the teacher having several opportunities to assist the writer with suggestions, corrections and additional ideas. Teachers and students can thus use provisionality to make their interchanges active ways of improving meaning.

The second example concerns the 'provisions' used in making a text. A text, as a first draft, is initially like a musical improvisation, made up from what is in the writer's textual resources. In a sense, some kind of text must come into existence in the mind, perhaps as what we would loosely call an idea; if you ask a student what they are going to write about they will usually have perhaps a vague notion. For some texts, far more planning is possible and desirable. In all cases the 'text in the head' takes on a manageable meaning as it is written down. Writers then turn their improvisation into a composition by reworking and strengthening their texts, partly through improving the use of their own textual matter and partly by using other texts to strengthen their own. For example, a literary essay is usually judged by how well the writers have incorporated parts of the original, i.e. quotations, into their text and explained their relevance. A student might now work on a split screen, composing their literary essay while reading and copying across from the original to illustrate their argument. A teacher might then respond to the student's text on a split screen, writing suggestions and ideas alongside the student's; the networked electronic medium also allows the teacher to send such suggestions to the whole class, to an individual or to groups with particular needs. Finally the teacher (and students) can store examples of work for the future which other students can refer to and actively use.

Some readers may instantly worry about plagiarism: will students ever write an original essay again? Well actually, they never did. First, all teachers teach them something; second, students talk to each other; and third, students often consult other sources. In fact, the more mature they get, the more sources they are supposed to consult and acknowledge. There is, of course, a genuine issue over plagiarism, which is that one printed text looks like another; there is no authentication possible in the print that is no longer a manuscript. However, students, as all teachers know, have always borrowed and copied each other's work. The teacher's real judgement comes through knowledge of the writer and the writer's voice. A good literary essay uses many voices; the essayist attempts to weave in the voice of the text, and of other commentators, to create a kind of vocal tapestry, the writer's artistry being judged by the extent to which the pattern is clear and consistent. In some other cultures, writers engage in such tapestries where the other voices are actually more important than their own; this is a different stance to the western tradition, which offers a challenge to our established ways of thinking. It also reminds us that in western culture in the past, imitation was a perfectly acceptable form of art.

When plagiarism is a deliberate masquerading of one writer's work as another's then this is simply stealing, an unethical use of another's property. I have every faith in teachers to teach children that this is wrong and to deal suitably directly with students who deliberately steal the work of others. However, provisionality means that writers will borrow even more and more effectively than in the past and this has every likelihood of making their texts better and in making them better writers. In composing an essay, the provisionality of the electronic text allows the student to incorporate, much more consciously, the texts of others and to manipulate these 'textites' (little bits of other text) into their own. Returning to my first point, the teacher as respondent has a similar opportunity to interact with the student's text, and within the text, to help improve it. Provisionality, put simply, means, potentially at least, an ongoing dialogue between writer (student) and reader (teacher) about improvability. It also makes the teacher's (writer) written response a text that the student (re-reader) can actively incorporate into the revised text. Readers may feel that this not only sounds very time-consuming but also requires an electronic interactivity based on individual machines and highly sophisticated networks. That situation would be ideal. However, as long as there is at least one machine and plenty of floppy discs, teachers and students can now experiment with this use of interactive composing. For those concerned with this as a potential distraction from proper 'pen and paper' writing, producing literate citizens and so on, the above way of working is already the norm in most large public and private organizations.

A final example in this section on composing illustrates how technology facilitates potentially more developmental uses of writing and it can be derived from the example of 'collective' writing above. Collaborative composing is an extremely difficult task. Most activities that I discuss in my final chapter are collaborative, but they almost always provide students with existing text and activities to undertake where 'two heads are better than one'. Composing text collaboratively 'from scratch' is not only very difficult but it may also be extremely frustrating, producing more tension and possibly bland writing. It is therefore a particular challenge requiring social skills and sensitivity, but probably manageable with a reasonable and supportive adult on hand. However, the kind of text I have in mind has a different genesis.

Human beings try to produce collective texts that attempt to 'speak for' groups, where the 'we' of the text attempts to express a consensual view. All such texts are prone to the cynical dismissal that they actually represent no one and that they are a bland elision of real differences. Nevertheless, they are also brave attempts to articulate a view that a group can subscribe to at that time: examples are manifestos, policies, 'public' letters, brochures, guides, etc. Using 'old' technology I used to ask students in their first year at secondary school to produce a guide to secondary life for primary children in their final year. The guide consisted of a slide show with a synchronized taped commentary, researched and written by groups of children. It was written, quite deliberately, as an alternative guide to the 'school' version. Rather surprisingly, or possibly disappointingly, it actually became a regular feature of the familiarization day for future students, being shown regularly for some years. More seriously, it was an alternative guide, more in the sense of providing the youngest students in the school with a chance to have 'their' say. It was a collaborative and collective enterprise: the writers had to adopt a generalized way of communicating, i.e. 'we' think 'you' ought to know this.

The opportunity for a group of children, anything from three to many more, but let us say a class of 30, to produce at least one such collective text seems to me a valuable learning experience, and one made far more powerful and easier, so therefore more manageable, through technology. It is an ideal task for the English classroom, demanding high-level input from potentially all children. It would be quite possible now for children to produce such a text, a guide to their school or a critical commentary on their local environment. There are many possibilities. This could be assembled by students researching and writing up sections which are edited into a whole text, reread and revisions suggested by all the contributors, with a final version produced as a document. Such an approach is made infinitely easier and more satisfying through the computer.

My example above was a 'mixed media' approach; now a multi-media outcome is truly possible – in later years I moved on to a video, with voice-over and written handouts, still 'mixed media'. The potential for students to be multi-media authors is now a reality. My students had to take photographs and choose the best, which I then converted into slides. Current students can also take photos but on a digital camera. They can shoot video footage and select both sequences and stills from it. They can 'capture' existing material via a scanner or a camera and use and/or edit it to their own ends. Their guide to the school might now contain masses of material for their primary audience to enjoy; it can even be interactive. The real challenge for these multi-media authors is to design material that helps and teaches their readers by setting up interactive opportunities. These might be appropriately serious, inviting the readers to experience a 'typical' day at secondary school, going to each lesson, being 'in' the playground and the dining hall, going home and trying homework. More playfully, readers might play the 'Are you a model pupil?' game, or they might try the 'Twenty myths about secondary school: true or false?' quiz. The cliché that technology makes learning fun also happens to be true. I would be surprised if English teachers found any of this threatening; so much of such an activity fits closely with current models of good practice. In designing a developmental English curriculum it would seem appropriate to me for teachers to undertake at least one such large-scale project each year with each year group that they teach. There is no reason why such a text might not be an interactive poetry anthology or, in a few years, a hypertext narrative. It would also seem extremely probable that the school's website will become the focus for much of this work.

GO FORTH AND MULTIPLY; TEXTUAL PRODUCTION AND REPRODUCTION

To make a metaphorical link with the previous section, just as texts are 'composed' so, in the natural world, do they 'decompose'. As physical objects they decay: as any visit to a second-hand bookshop will affirm, decaying old texts have their own peculiar scent. Metaphorically, however, some texts refuse to die: they remain paradoxically alive; defying time's ravages, readers lovingly keep them alive. Some preservative institutions keep them in a kind of formaldehyde, a cultural aspic or amber, so that they may be taken off the shelf and examined, rather like an extinct species. This metaphor might be helpful in reminding us that English teachers in some countries have had this role thrust upon them. However, what good English teachers do, in that well-worn but crucial phrase, is bring texts 'alive' in the classroom. They refuse the antiseptic, 'Don't touch that text with your dirty hands' approach and make their students roll up their sleeves and mess up the text. In this way each student can put the text back together and, to stretch my metaphor a little further, can re-animate it, give it a new lease of life because as a living reader it 'lives' in them. My research over a decade (Goodwyn, 1992; Goodwyn and Findlay, 1999) shows that English teachers hold firm to the belief that literature remains at the centre of their work and that the purpose of interacting with literature is life-affirming.

In the future English curriculum, that most practical aspect of 'old' technology, the book, will remain at the centre. However, the living text, the text that survives beyond the natural life of the object/text, is now available for us. In parallel the living element of each student-produced text is similarly free from the dreadful physical restraints of the awful 'exercise' book, still the dominating channel for written expression in many schools, in the UK at least. I offer here some approaches that are currently available to most teachers, and some that are very close to realization.

The advent of the CD-Rom is just beginning to help students enjoy literature in new and distinct ways. At the simplest level a CD version of a book can be powerfully enriched by visual resources that enthuse and support readers. A reader, or group of readers, can examine a text and can call up, when they want to, some extra information or illustration. I would argue that this initially mimics that remarkable text 'the scholarly edition'; current readers will have strong memories of such texts where the notes took up sometimes 90 per cent of a Shakespeare page. However, the notes were there, needed or not. A good textual CD already has layers of resources, linked in ways that allow readers to pursue textual and thematic issues in depth as they wish. If a student is reading *Great Expectations* and suddenly wants to know whether the boy Pip is based on Dickens himself, then it is possible to search instantly for some evidence of this in the text's additional resources. Some may argue that this is somehow 'too easy': students will not learn to search properly through indexes. This essentially misses the point. All textual apparatus is designed to help readers understand a text; one must also learn how to use the apparatus – the more useful an apparatus the more it will be used. Many students are already far quicker in grasping the way to use such texts than their teachers. Such instant help is actually much closer to how we think, and a good CD text will also allow us to trace our inquiries; we can look back over our reading and examine what we wanted to know and what we have found. Teachers will soon be able to review their students' reading patterns and so have some overview of the kind and extent of such readings; this is invaluable information.

We have only begun to glimpse the possibilities offered by technology for bringing all kinds of texts closer to students. As more and more collections of texts are organized as databases, either on CDs or as websites, so the possibilities for students to research and extend their knowledge increase. Major authors, especially those out of copyright, are often now available on a single CD or website in ways that would have made even the richest library envious a few years ago. Vast anthologies of poems are now available in ways that make them seem small and manageable. Students with disabilities will soon be enabled to ask for a reading of a text or for a braille version to be printed. Even more extraordinarily, students will be able to produce an edition themselves of an important text. That text might be a collection of Shakespeare's sonnets or it might be an anthology of their own poetry with commentary and illustrations.

Ultimately, we will all be able to experiment and play with textual language in intriguing ways. One of the more enjoyable elements in literary criticism of recent years has been the advent of 'playfulness' towards texts. The adoption of this playful stance is not to be confused with a trivializing, or a merely ridiculing, reading. Its essence lies in the discovery that texts offer all readers space and gaps to 'fill'; texts invite readers to consider what has been left out and the temptation is to 'put it in'. Inviting our students to 'play' with existing texts (see my final chapter) asks them to read closely and discover more about that particular text and texts in general. I offer, therefore, a simple list of 'messing about' activities as illustration. What happens if:

- You run a spell-check over a page of Shakespeare?
- You run a British spell-check over an 'American' story?
- You take a paragraph of Henry James and 'Hemingway' it into short sentences?
- You take a bawdy paragraph from Chaucer and put 'modern' rude words in to replace the 'old' ones?

- You take the opening of a novel and present it as a newspaper article with columns and headlines?
- You take two short poems and randomly mix them up?
- You try to take the irony out of a Jane Austen paragraph?
- You take a conventional poem by Wordsworth and 'e. e. cummings' it, or vice versa?

In each case a 'new' text is created with an intertextual link to another. I feel quite confident that our students will themselves 'invent' new textual strategies which we will enjoy and value alongside them.

IT'S A MAILWORLD

Users of e-mail have already discovered that its essential problem is that it reveals not only how people love to communicate but that they often send messages just to communicate; nothing meaningful occurs. However, the astonishing facility of e-mail is turning us all into rather better, if somewhat promiscuous, correspondents.

The serious value to teachers is already evident. It is now possible to link with students from around the world and establish either specific or ongoing projects that have powerful educational value. This is an essential aspect of e-mail that will remain important. Sending letters around the world was always quite slow and cumbersome although it retains its own value and may yet re-emerge as a special form of communication.

It is not just the speed and reciprocity of e-mail that enhances learning; it is also the medium itself. It is a new hybrid form of communication that brings speech and writing together, inviting conversational writing with a voice that the reader will soon 'hear'. It encourages groups to discuss and debate issues that they are interested in; these electronic communities can have long or short lives, inclusive or exclusive membership. In other words e-mail is a linguistic and symbolic phenomenon, something for students to examine and reflect upon as well as use. They will also need help in recognizing how much e-mail junk they will need to jettison in their lives if they are to have time to read what is meaningful.

With e-mails come attachments. An attachment allows a student to send a text to another student, in the next room or on the other side of the world. Such a text might be a rough draft inviting the reader to comment or write in the text. It might be a project, crafted over many months and offered as a definitive statement from that individual or their class; for example, with the best technical facilities this might be a thorough account, using photos and video clips, of what life is like for teenagers in their particular community. It might be a documentary account of those students' lives, prepared for a peer audience growing up in what might be a very different culture and geography. However, there are currently plenty of technical difficulties associated with such use of attachments and there are the dangers mentioned above when unscrupulous computer-users deliberately disguise infected material which then severely damages its trusting host. This is a technical and ethical issue which our students will soon be aware of.

E-mail and its uses are already well established, except in most schools. Soon schools will be electronic communities with internal and external websites. This will change communication and representation in everyday school life in ways we can predict and in ways that will surprise us. Not all such changes will be 'good' in the sense that neither we nor our students are all good; young people will become even more adept at playing with adult systems and in subverting them; in other words some things will never change.

VIRTUAL AND VIRTUOUS ENGLISH; TEACHERS AND STUDENTS IN COLLABORATION

The subsequent chapters in this collection illustrate some of the current, innovative developments in English and provide us with ideas for the very near future. I shall conclude this opening chapter with a brief examination of the learner–teacher relationship in the emergent digital age.

This collection is published, without irony, as a book. Students and teachers of English have been sharing books together since the subject came into being; they have also been arguing and debating about books. However, for many students the much-vaunted claims of English, to encourage a love of reading and respect for books, remain a form of fiction. This does not reflect on the books themselves, and rarely would it be fair to condemn ourselves as teachers; we have worked in very adverse circumstances in places where encouraging reading is frequently impossible. So teaching English is often a struggle, virtuous and worthy, but sometimes depressingly ineffective if measured by the very demanding criteria mentioned above.

It is much too soon to overplay the impact of technology on learning in school. It is much easier to demonstrate how technology is transforming activities in the home, some of which include more learning by children and adolescents, and, excitingly, adults. I strongly disagree with the view that schools will soon be redundant, however. English teachers in the study described above (Goodwyn *et al.*, 1997) were asked to imagine their classrooms in ten or so years in the future. Generally they saw them as better resourced, containing perhaps six to eight work-stations around the room, retaining easily moved chairs and tables. They imagined one teacher and a class of children working more flexibly than now but still concerned with a common aim and paying attention to a topic worth studying. This is both a somewhat conservative view and also a perfectly reasonable one based on the very slow pace of change in schools.

However, this unadorned vision has two key principles at its heart. The first is the role of the teacher. A good teacher is irreplaceable and that term 'good' has both the effective, and the moral, dimension. Almost all English teachers are currently relatively unskilled users of technology; this will steadily change and new forms of pedagogy will emerge as teachers skillfully implement ways to help their students make better progress. The re-skilling of teachers will reduce their anxieties and will also allow them to bring 'virtually' anything they want into the classroom as a learning resource; this signals a great change. It makes teachers more powerful, allowing them to adjust the learning of their groups to keep them interested and collaborating, negotiating with the teacher rather than competing. This change will become evident in every subject, not just in English.

Such changes to classroom resources and practices also re-endorse each teacher's essentially moral role as a guardian. I have touched on some of the dangers that technology brings with it; it is not just discs that can be corrupted, human beings can be too. Students working under the guidance of a trusted adult remains our best model of learning. Tennyson's 'Ulysses' is full of praise for his crew; they undertook their voyages together. Students will themselves be less of a crew and more of a community, freer and more powerful than in the past, but I do not see them incessantly hunched over an individual screen; they will, as now, want to turn to a neighbour and say 'Wow, look what I am learning', or even more likely, 'Look what I have found for us.' Those children who want to spend all their time hunched over a screen are foolish; they need an adult to 'unhunch' them. It is not necessarily that teacher always knows best but that the teacher is both more knowing and better at judging what is best; I am convinced that technology will never replace the experience gained from trying to help students learn, although it shows real signs of supporting and enhancing that experience. Future English teachers, experienced with students' learning and with technology as a part of that (and crucially their own) learning will have even greater potential than now to create learning communities; communities that feel secure, secure enough to take risks and to challenge conventional wisdom as well as to listen to it.

English teachers themselves, as a community, will become remarkably good at using technology, just as they are remarkably good now at using texts to help students learn. A text, such as a narrative poem like 'Ulysses', takes us into a virtual world; there is no text for an individual reader until that individual has engaged with the text, then the text takes on a new life, both 'out there' as a real text, as part of the actual world and 'in here', part of my world; yet paradoxically that text will, almost certainly, outlive me and my own inner, virtual world. In other words, English teachers have been working with this much-vaunted 'virtual' reality stuff all along and doing very well with it. The advent of more 'virtuality', especially in its emerging forms, provides us with exciting scope to do even better; we may never arrive at 'the Happy Isles' but the journey to a newer world begins to look inviting.

Chapter 2

Framing and Design in ICT in English: Towards a New Subject and New Practices in the Classroom

RICHARD ANDREWS

I want in this chapter to look into the future of ICT in English, predicting as best I can what English (or language arts) will look like in five years' time. Ten or twenty years would be too far, given the pace of change, but in five years we can imagine in England and Wales another review of the National Curriculum and, more optimistically, a fully operational National Grid for Learning, well-integrated lifelong learning from cradle to grave and Internet access in every school and home. In five years' time most of us as teachers will still be responsible for the learning of children and young people, of our own children and grandchildren – not forgetting our own learning. Furthermore, by 2002 almost all English teachers at primary and secondary levels in the UK will have undergone training in the application of ICT in their subject,[1] similar moves being under way in many other English-speaking countries. Part of the purpose of this chapter then, is to anticipate the context in which English teachers will find themselves in the middle of the next decade, and to identify good practice, that is likely to have a higher profile in the next few years. In order to look to the future, we need to see how far we have come in the last fifteen years or so, and what the state of play is at present.

The best review of the last fifteen years in England and Wales is by Sally Tweddle in her article 'A retrospective: fifteen years of computers in English'. This article originally took the form of an address to a colloquium organized in 1997 at the start of the IT in English project (see Stannard 1997). In it she reflected on the period since 1980. In the 1980s, despite some good software like Bob Moy's 'Developing Tray' (a superb cloze approach where the students had to make a text rise to the surface of the screen, like a print in a developing tray), the major application of computers in the classroom was in word processing. Because word processing is second nature to us now in our personal and professional lives (whereas, ironically, pupils in schools are still writing in exercise books), it is easy to take for granted what digital composing has done for us. It has enabled concentration on the major structuring of writing; enabled argument, report and information writing to have a better medium for their expression than pen and paper; encouraged collaboration and talk about writing at the screen; liberated and validated drafting and editing; and improved presentation.

On the down side, it has also made many learners dependent upon spell- and grammar-checkers; been over-rated in its effect on narrative writing; limited a sense of the whole work through its window on to text; and, in some cases, led to a deterioration in handwriting quality. Although, as English teachers, we worry about such developments, they are perhaps inevitable as a new technology pervades practice in schools, homes and the workplace. Just as calculators have changed the emphasis of what is necessary and possible in Mathematics, so too the word processor and multi-media portable are changing the dynamics of English. What Frank Smith (1980) calls the 'secretarial' skills – the surface skills of accuracy and presentation in handwritten work – will change in nature and allow children to focus more on the 'compositional' skills of invention, arrangement and expression.

As with the Technical and Vocational Education Initiative in the UK of the 1980s (which brought the first computers into the English classroom), English teachers were slow to take up the challenge of computers in the curriculum. Innovation has been patchy, sometimes driven by government projects (ESG IT Scheme, 1988; Project Gemini, 1990; CD-Rom and Interactive Video, 1992; Portables in Schools, 1993; CD-Rom primary, 1994; the Superhighways initiative, 1995; IT in English, 1995–98). The problem hasn't been so much to do with a Luddite tendency on the part of English teachers and primary school language specialists – though the subversive, humanities-based, liberal and book-dominated culture of English (the orthodoxy since the 1920s) – is undoubtedly a factor in the resistance of English teachers to new technologies. Rather, it has been more to do with short-termism on the part of government, though a critical momentum in the use of ICT in the classroom has been reached in the last two years through the spread of multi-media portables, the development of the National Grid for Learning and the training of all teachers in ICT applications in the classroom.

Although progress has, on the whole, been fitful, some of it has been inspirational. At the same colloquium at which Tweddle spoke three years ago, the other keynote speaker was Richard Lanham, the author of *The Electronic Word*. He amazed everyone with pyrotechnics from his keyboards, suggesting that writing was to be more 3D, more like choreography, more interactive, more multimodal. He also suggested that multi-media was hardly new, and illustrated his point with reference to medieval illuminated manuscripts, e.g. a canonical text surrounded by commentary from an authority, in turn surrounded by students' annotations, and all interspersed with fine illustration. In other words, an early multi-levelled and multi-media hypertext. Lanham's work is particularly interesting because his own development – from professor of literary education and rhetoric to a passionate interest in new media and their role in democracies – has entailed a review of the history of the relationship between the visual and verbal in communication (see Andrews and Simons, 1996).

Whereas Lanham's focus was on the history of multi-media, my focus has been on ICT in schools, in education: what has happened and is happening there? One shining example of multi-media work in a primary school has been the Rosendale Odyssey project. This project, which ran for a number of years in Rosendale Primary School in Brixton, London, brought together photographers, artists, researchers, teachers and schoolchildren aged 5 to 7 in an attempt to create a website to celebrate a hundred years of the school's history. In line with current good practice, pupils were asked to research their parents' and grandparents' stories, to seek out archival material, to experiment with taking and making photographs (both conventionally and digitally), and to write new material. Stories were written, photographs taken and experimented with digitally as well as being used to explore their visual possibilities through extension of the images in drawing and painting. Photomontage, caption-writing, oral storytelling, the making of displays and exhibitions, presentations to parents and others in the community – all these and more were put together with the help of artists, and the result is a vibrant, readable, engaging resource (see Photographers' Gallery, 1997). Since the project's artists and researchers left in the summer of 1997, the teachers have continued the work in the school, having learnt new skills in website design and management. The key point, however, is that exciting new forms of expression grew from what is considered good practice within language work, but took this practice in a direction that fully acknowledged the visual dimension.

In terms of software the picture is still pretty grim, but the prospects are good and some excellent products are beginning to come on to the market. First, the general picture. In June 1997 the DfEE commissioned from the IT in English group an extensive review of software for curriculum use in English. This was born from an anxiety in government circles that, first, if the British community didn't move quickly in the production of good software for schools, it would be swamped by global material, and second, that something substantial would have to be produced to supply the National Grid for Learning. The problem was exacerbated by the fact that Acorn- and BBC-generated software became increasingly remote from IBM, Microsoft and Apple Macintosh standard ware. The IT in English group commissioned the review and a filleted version is included in *A Review of Software for Curriculum Use* (NCET, 1997b). This is not much use for teachers, as all the references to particular products and companies have been edited out. The full version is available from Actis (1997) and is, as yet, unpublished.

Here are some brief quotations from the report, which give an accurate picture of the present state of play for ages 7 to 14:

Web design tools specifically for children need to be developed further.

A noticeable gap in more recent output is that devoted to creative work.

Text analysis and search tools need to be developed that address the specific needs of English teachers, faced with the instant availability of so many texts in electronic form and the increasing emphasis on grammar.

There is a shortage of imaginative UK-based software that explores literature other than Shakespeare.

Most spelling programs are poor.

Distinctive software does exist, for example in The English and Media Centre's *Picture Power* and the British Film Institute's *Backtracks* (both CD-Roms). *Picture Power* (1997) works with still images, inviting the reader/ composer to arrange and rearrange them in montages, with captions and music. *Backtracks* (1997) is an educational resource for understanding the moving image, also in relation to music, words and narrative. Other good examples are 20th Century Fox's educational CD-Rom *Great Expectations*, based on Alfonso Cuaron's recent modern-day film version of the novel; as well as the many CD-Roms on Shakespeare's plays.

In the light of such developments in the last fifteen years, the future of ICT in English can be addressed in two parts: first through policy and the likely role of government; and then through a look at how practice might develop. I won't dwell on technological change, except to say at the outset that the various modes of communication (e.g. video, text, image), and all the diverse equipment dealing with different modes of delivery and information storage, will be integrated in a single delivery system available in home and school.

There are a number of government initiatives that have taken place, and are taking place, around the turn of the century. They are the TTA's Initial Teacher Training National Curriculum for the Use of ICT in Subject Teaching resulting in a Circular (4/98), which has set the standard for new entrants to teaching as well as for existing teachers; the DfEE's plan to use Lottery funding through the New Opportunities Fund initiative to train all existing teachers in the use of ICT; the DfEE/BECTa (formerly NCET)'s Multimedia Portables for Teachers project; the IT in English project, which is one of a number of subject-based IT projects; the National Grid for Learning; 'The Learning Age', the government's initiative on lifelong learning. Coupled with technological advances and the moves by big companies to equip each school and library with Internet access, as well as the drift towards increased use of the computer in the home, where are these developments taking us?

The following picture is emerging: in 1999 there was the launch of a continuing professional development, or INSET, programme for teachers in ICT in subject teaching, not necessarily delivered by, but certainly accreditable by, universities, which follows closely the TTA's standards and guidelines on improving subject expertise; subject-focused ICT development; and perhaps the provision of a multi-media portable for each teacher so they can plug into the Internet (especially the National Grid for Learning) at home or at school. As far as teachers' own development and qualifications are concerned, there will be a standardization of attainment levels post-degree, so that you can move from PGCE to Masters to MPhil/PhD, or to the professional doctorates like the EdD or generic DProf. If two other government initiatives are anything to go by – The Institute for Learning and Teaching, to improve lecturers' teaching powers; and the Individual Learning Accounts idea – professional development will almost become a must, and teachers will be seen as crucial to the whole enterprise. It is important to cite the above developments, which empower schools and teachers to influence the nature of their subject and the way it is taught, and thus give them more agency in the first decade of the twenty-first century than they had in the top-down, assessment-driven 1990s. To begin to consider more practical issues, what is the creative potential of ICT in English, and the application of it in the classroom and school?

The use of text – of words – on the computer screen is changing fast. Whereas in the printed book, particularly in fiction, the words are often ascetically – to give room for the imagination – framed by the cool white margins, on the computer screen they are conventionally framed in 'windows' alongside, beneath or above visual images, icons, navigation tools, text in different fonts, etc. The same is the case in some textbooks, comics, magazines and, increasingly, in newspapers, *viz* that visual images and words are contiguous and battling each other or complementing each other in gaining the reader's attention. This is not the case with illustrations to text in fiction, which are subsidiary to the text. It is not that we are leaving words behind and are 'turning to the visual'; simply that the visual is coming up alongside the verbal again in communication. My first practical point, then, is that the verbal is no longer the only mode we have to deal with as English and language teachers. The same is true, perhaps less obviously, with sound. Such new skills are not to be assumed; they require training, so that the employment of the visual and/or aural alongside the written text (for writing and reading purposes) is not a pale imitation of what might be possible in Art or Music, but draws on the best of what is possible in those subjects. English and language teachers will have to develop better skills in design and composition, but at the same time will need to look to colleagues who are trained in the visual and sonic arts to collaborate on new compositions. Such collaboration is not new: the putting on of a school play has always required exactly such collaboration. But collaboration in the design of multi-media software or the interpretation of it *is* relatively new.

Second, we're moving away from the authority of the text as a stable, fixed, cultural artefact. We know the folio manuscript and the quarto manuscript of Shakespeare were hardly stable versions themselves – or were an attempt to record the various versions around at the time – but now you can play with Shakespeare, by, for example, intercutting his text with yours, editing his words, writing new speeches and lines, commenting alongside his words in the same font. In many ways, we are seeing the fruits of reader–response approaches that have been developing since the 1970s in which the reader is given more prominence in the making of meaning in relation to texts. For some time, different readings have enriched the business of literary appreciation, with a movement away from canonical New Critic and 'practical criticism' approaches; the authority of the text has diminished. There is more scope than ever for children's and students' voices to appear alongside established voices (see Morgan and Andrews, 1999), and the more interactivity in software programming becomes sophisticated, the more accessible this kind of dialogue is going to become. In such a world, reading becomes a creative act, and the processes of composition apply to both reading and writing, interpreting and making.

A third point is that writing is becoming more like speech. E-mail is a good example. Exchanges are dialogic, often informal. The predominance of e-mail, not only in business communication but increasingly in personal communication, has meant a quickening of communicative responses, and generally a shortening of response time and of the messages sent. This does not mean to say that formal genres and text-types in writing are necessarily becoming more speech-like; just that the preponderance and expansion of speech-like forms of writing is continuing apace.

Fourth, the creative act is not only writing, but what Gunther Kress calls 'design' (Kress, 1997) or what might be termed more fundamentally 'composition': the putting together of existing text, images and sounds with new text, images and sound in a collage-like way within cultural 'frames' (or by breaking or transgressing those frames). Again, teachers have been designing brochures with classes, using posters, reviewing books and displaying these reviews for some time. This kind of work is likely to increase, with a number of media and different skills being involved in the creation of each artefact. The skills are not only important to develop in themselves; but the *integration* of such skills is what learning to read and write is about.

To give another example from the Rosendale Odyssey project: one of the most engaging elements of the website is the 'hair tips' stack. Here the children put aerial and profile photographs of their heads and hairstyles alongside descriptions of how they comb their hair and how their styles have changed over the years. The writing is fluent, witty, knowledgeable, confident and full of authorial 'voice' (Graves, 1982). Each description is completed with a 'hair tip', e.g. 'Don't cut your hair short unless you're really sure about what you're doing 'cos it takes a long time to grow again.' In most cases the writing and photographs are accompanied by the speaking voice of the child on the audio track.

What are the school and classroom implications of these changes in the way the subject is approached? One is that we can expect further crossing of subject boundaries. I've written elsewhere (Andrews, 1996) that Art, English and IT – we should also include Music – are converging on the computer screen. And those boundaries need to be crossed, because what teachers often receive from pupils is good writing accompanied by poor illustration; or vice versa. Why can't we have good writing and good visuals alongside each other? The curriculum will be very impoverished if we find ourselves concentrating in

ROSENDALE ODYSSEY PROJECT: HAIR TIPS

 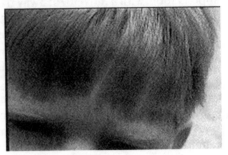

Hello my name is Luke. I have quite short, straight blond hair and lots of nice orangy freckles. When I was a baby, I had red hair but now it's blond. It changed colour slowly and I hope it's stopped because I like the colour of my hair how it is now. I get it cut about every three weeks near Blackheath in a barbers. I get it done with my dad, he takes me there. I like going to get it cut because I don't want it to grow long. My dad has his hair cut as well, he has the same hair cut as me. I get it washed before I get it cut and they put spray in it too. It smells of perfume and it smells nice. I put gel in my hair to make it look nice.
LUKE'S HAIR TIP: It is good to wear a hat in the summer to stop your neck from being sunburnt.

My name is Michaela and I like playing on the helicopter. I have got long browny-gold hair. It is not thick hair, it's fine. I have it in lots of different styles. I have it in plaits, french plaits, pigtails and ponytails. I only wear headbands and sometimes a flower. My auntie did my french plait and my mum does the other things, I like french plaits. I would like to learn how to do french plaits and my mum needs to be taught how to do them. She does them alright at the top but she can't tie them properly. I don't have my hair cut I have it trimmed. They just do the dead ends. I don't have any dead ends. My hair isn't easy to brush in the morning, my mum brushes it for me and it sometimes hurts. In the night it all tangles up.
MICHAELA'S HAIR TIP: If you have long hair or short hair up to your shoulders you have to brush your hair before you go to bed because if you don't, it gets tangled.

'literacy hours' on words only, particularly if Art and the other arts are sidelined or squeezed from the curriculum altogether.

In short, we need to build on the strengths of English teaching: its creativity; its exploration of different forms and genres; its embracing of Drama and the other arts; its long tradition of giving voice to the personal; its often subversive, culturally aware presence in the curriculum. At the same time, the configuration of the subject in the curriculum seems now inadequate to the demands of the present in terms of written, off-line and on-line communication. There needs to be a new conception of the subject at primary and secondary levels that moves away from any of the prevalent models of the 1980s or 1990s. In terms of the development of the subject, new thinking might run along the lines set out in this manifesto-like statement (Andrews and Reid, 1998):

> We wish to propose a group that will look in the medium- and long-term at the possibilities for integration of the verbal, visual and aural in communication through ICT. We are reacting to what we see as a fossilization of impermeable and static subject boundaries that are to be reinforced by the light/small-scale review of the National Curriculum that will take place in 1999/2000. We are concerned that the continued presence of the current curriculum subjects areas is preventing commerce between them, preventing exploration of the creative potential of new technologies, and rapidly getting out of touch with what is happening in the wider world. The English curriculum is in danger of being left behind.
>
> We also feel that there is a danger that the use of ICT is determined by the possibility of access, rather than by ideas or any rationale of its use.
>
> We are not proposing another cross-curricular initiative that works with existing subjects. Rather, we see a need for a new configuration that brings together the expressive, the communicative and the creative through ICT: in short, a new curriculum area in which making, composing, reading (in the broadest sense), speaking and listening are foregrounded – not for their own sake but in the service of real world ends both within the communities within school, and in the communities in which identities are formed beyond the school. There is potential in the new kinds of literacy – informed by the World Wide Web, the 'turn to the visual', increasing access at home and at school to multimedia and to digital broadcast technologies – to build a flexible and relevant curriculum that answers the needs of children, students and adults in the twenty-first century.
>
> What's more, we need to ground creativity in social contexts, seeing learning as transformative in personal, social and political ways rather than measuring learning in terms of competences, skills or capabilities or indeed by conceiving of movement between the various art forms as 'transferable'. We are concerned that the arts are being further marginalized by current curricular thinking.

We see ICT as underpinning an enhanced and richer conception of literacy that brings together the verbal and the visual, the aural and the choreographic. We see ICT as enabling new possible contexts for these forms of expression, as bringing about a return to a close relationship between the various modes of communication, and as liberating creativity both in and outside the classroom.

There are opportunities to reshape the curriculum in ways that are currently being hinted at by new specialist schools and colleges, for example by opening up the timetable, by integrating different subjects, by allowing ICT to pervade curricular work and by creating specific briefs for students which demand research, the interpretation and reintegration of information, and the exploration of new audiences. In this last respect, schooling will have much in common with current and future movements in the arts and arts education in which alternative audiences and locations are sought, and which in turn bring about new art forms.

Pedagogically too, we feel that we need to push things forward, rather than assume that current curricular programmes have all the answers. All too often, conservatism in curriculum reinforces conservatism and transmission ideologies in teaching and learning. Indeed, we would argue that to maximise learning potential, we need to reconfigure the curriculum to make space for young people to find their own (multiple) identities in a number of communities, and to engage in communication in a number of media. The new technologies will provide opportunities for learning of which we are, as yet, unaware.

Another challenge is that we must seek increasingly good software. One example of a group of English teachers who have set up a business in software design is Actis, the group based in Derbyshire. They not only design software; they also review it and act as the interface between the electronic worlds and the world of language and English teaching, e.g. through in-service training for teachers. Until now, much of the software for language teaching has been written by computer-driven people whose sensibilities are driven by fancy rather than by imagination. Somehow they seem not to have grown up: obsessed by dungeons and dragons, excited by buttons, and captivated by closed-off routes through material. The material is often initially engaging, but soon runs out of imaginative momentum as all that seems to be offered is the reduction of a literary text to little more than a crossword puzzle.

Yet another implication is that classrooms and ways of working in them will gradually change. Schools themselves will not disappear quickly – certainly not in five years – but I can see the learning agenda, preferred learning styles, the 'learning template' outstripping what goes on in schools. There is an interesting and difficult tension to be resolved between the layout and overall function of schools on the one hand, and the nature of learning on the other. Perhaps, even in five years, schools will take on more of the community role that many of them have been playing since the 1960s. One secondary school in the north of England plans to change its relationship with learners over the next few years via multi-media portable computers. It sees children and other lifelong learners operating for much of their time away from the school premises, being part of electronic communities that meet from time to time in school for particular purposes; it therefore sees a radical transformation taking place in the school day and, in due course, it sees itself as becoming superfluous to the formal process of school education as we have known it. Such developments depend very much on who owns or appropriates the concept 'lifelong learning', the debate on which, until now, has largely left schools out; on the way government initiatives like the University for Industry develop; and on developments in the understanding of and practice in learning design.

What implications are there for English teachers at primary and secondary levels? In practice, will children submit homework on disc, or directly to the teacher's computer via e-mail? Will computer conferencing establish itself more centrally in education and learning? Will teachers download ready-made lesson plans from the Internet or the National Grid for Learning? The answer is probably yes; and indeed such practice is already under way. But will the school day change? Probably not. Will the curriculum and the relationship between teacher and student change? The combination of millennium fever, and a rising sense that the National Curriculum template and various adjustments of it since 1988 don't suit teachers, schools or children and society's needs, may well force a breakthrough in the next five years. It could be that the prevalent model for English teaching over the last thirty or so years (see Goodwyn and Findlay, in press), namely the 'personal growth' model, might find renewed confirmation in the inevitably more individualized learning that will ensue. Learners will determine their own routes through material, and choose their own material from banks of resources readily available on CD-Rom or on the Internet, via local libraries as well as through schools. ICT therefore might build on the strengths that English teachers see as central to their subject. Other models of English teaching, such as those based on cultural heritage, skills-based curricula or cultural studies, will be seen as aspects of 'English' (if we retain the term) that the learner can access to further his or her own learning development. In short, then, the transformation that English as a subject will have brought about in the last quarter of the twentieth century will be more about learning style and orientation than about the subject itself.

In terms of teacher development, what is likely to work best in terms of teachers getting up to speed on ICT? The most obviously successful INSET approach of all the projects I mentioned above has been that of the Multimedia Portables for Teachers project. Of the teachers involved in the pilot, 91 per cent successfully used CD-Roms; 76 per cent successfully used the World Wide Web; 62 per cent successfully used e-mail. To quote from the evaluation (Harrison, 1997):

- One set of colleagues shared a machine so they were able to write reports on the computer at home as well as a school.
- One teacher used e-mail to contact friends, deliver a report and exchange draft graphic designs. He also joined an on-line education debate.
- One school discovered that the portable was invaluable for enabling pupils to catch up on missed work, particularly when used in conjunction with an appropriate CD-Rom.
- One teacher found that using the portable for word-processing work with a small, low-ability group, increased pupils' motivation and achievement.

In general, 93 per cent agreed that their use of ICT had increased substantially; 95 per cent agreed that the project had allowed them to develop their teaching; 90 per cent agreed that the school as a whole had benefited; 95 per cent agreed that the money spent on computers was worthwhile. There's a clear lesson here: give multi-media portables to the teachers and they will undertake their own INSET, particularly if driven by economic or strategic (on the part of senior management and governor) pressure.

In pedagogic terms, it seems that the CD-Rom is creating a niche for itself as a resource. It's robust, easy to use, fast and encylopaedic in range; able to contain still and moving images; shareable, portable. It is beginning to be used for storing creative work and for archival purposes as the technology becomes more accessible. The Internet is slower, but good for creative and ongoing work, and for research. To date it has been the least practicable medium for use in the classroom, but the technical and access problems are gradually being overcome. E-mail is fast, dialogic, a good compositional tool at distance. All the different electronic and digital media have their strengths and their weaknesses, as do the conventional formats of book, magazine, newspaper, TV and radio.

Individuals and groups are developing their own communication management and their own styles. Schools and classrooms will do the same, looking for an economy of media use that maximizes learning, is affordable and reliable. Once teachers are equipped with their own multi-media portables, they will be able to store and revise lessons plans, store school and LEA plans, government documents and records about their pupils in digital form in an easily accessible way. They will be able to project materials and lesson objectives or learning outcomes via video projectors to small, medium or large groups in school. Equally, pupils and students will be undertaking their own research, managing their own files, undertaking their own tasks and projects and submitting work for assessment electronically as well as in print and other forms.

Consider this scenario, in a primary or secondary school in about the year 2005: you, as teacher, arrive for the school day with your multi-media portable on your shoulder. Your 'lesson' with a Year 5 or Year 8 class is a rarer occasion than in the late twentieth century because the pupils have more time to themselves for research and preparation now. The main activity of the lesson is what you cannot easily replicate virtually: discussion, physical interaction, large-scale ritual and drama, community learning with questions coming from the learners rather than the teacher. Work is conveyed to the teacher's laptop via radio links between the computers in the room, so that wires are not necessary. One of the principal aims of the lesson is for the pupils to leave with a better sense of what it means to be a good learner in a particular subject.

The future is waiting there for us to make it work, rather than shaping us to its own commercial ends. In terms of schooling, it's going to be in the hands of the learners – the children themselves – urging a sharper sense of technological possibility from their teachers. On the teachers' part, widespread training over the first years of the new century, an increased confidence and knowledge in the use of ICT in English teaching and – not least – knowledge of the subject and where its boundaries can be creatively extended: these and other qualities will help guide children in gaining command of a wide range of media to be deployed in their writing.

ACKNOWLEDGEMENTS

I am grateful to Rebecca Sinker, researcher and artist, for permission to quote from the Rosendale Odyssey CD-Rom and for discussions on digital photography and English; to colleagues at Middlesex University, especially Howard Hollands, Victoria de Rijke, Peter Medway, Stephen Boyd-Davis, Barry Curtis and Karen Raney for raids on the interface of the verbal and visual; to Mark Reid of the British Film Institute; and to Colin Harrison and BECTa for permission to quote from the evaluation of the Multimedia Portables in Schools project.

NOTES

1   The Teacher Training Agency/New Opportunities Fund project to train the nation's teachers in the application of ICT in their subject teaching runs from 1999 to 2002, by which time all teachers are expected to be capable to the level of entrants to the profession, as set out in DfEE Circular 4/98. Providers of training were approved in early 1999, and training began in spring of that year.

Chapter 3

ICT in English:
Views from Northern Ireland

JUDE COLLINS

INTRODUCTION

> My name is Sarah. I am 20 and I am computer illiterate ... It might not
> seem possible in this era of the laptop-toting whizzkid, but there are a
> lot of us out there: students who have never learnt how to work a
> computer ...
>
> I have even been encouraged to hand-write essays by some tutors,
> on the premise that there is little point getting the creative juices
> flowing on a computer when in an exam you have to handwrite your
> answers. I could go through three years of university without ever
> typing an essay.
>
> (Sarah Laitner, 'No computers in our day', *The Guardian Higher
> Education*, 2 March 1999)

For those concerned with the development of ICT in schools, these comments
from a history student at Cambridge University deserve attention. The
increasing role of ICT in all our lives may be evident, but the danger remains
that we will overestimate the prevalence of ICT knowledge and skills. For
many in universities and schools, the confidence and familiarity needed for
successful use of ICT remains an aspiration rather than a reality. The
computing tide has not lifted all boats.

This chapter looks at the realities of ICT work for a number of student
teachers and practising teachers in Northern Ireland schools. It is hoped that
the classroom experiences described may provide comparison points for
teachers engaged in similar work. It is also hoped that reflection on the
comments and practice of these teachers will provide a basis for the formation
of ICT policy. To be effective, policy must be rooted in the day-to-day
experience of those who work in classrooms.

In its policy document *A Strategy for Education Technology in Northern*

Ireland (1997), the Department of Education for Northern Ireland (DENI) sounds a sober note. Despite the education service's best efforts over the past twenty years, 'we are still a considerable distance from seeing the effective integration of ICT into the curriculum and across all subjects' (DENI 1997, p. 8). The document concedes that while the inclusion of ICT as a compulsory Cross-Curricular Theme (CCT) in the Northern Ireland statutory curriculum in 1989 gave some fresh impetus to ICT, the slimming-down of programmes of study has meant a lessening of emphasis. The Department's judgement is based on factual evidence. Secondary school inspections during the 1994–6 period show little success in the integration of ICT into the secondary curriculum.

> ICT is generally underdeveloped in the majority of secondary English departments, even where there are strengths in other aspects of their provision. Insufficient access is often an impediment to use. In about a quarter of the sample, where ICT provision and/or access is good, the use of ICT is still poor. When word processors are used, the pupils usually compose by hand, and then type a fair copy on the computer, with little or no improvement to style, structure or content, even though redrafting is an important aspect of the programme of study. Relatively little effective use has been seen of recently-acquired CD-Rom reference titles; in some cases, the pupils copy text directly from the screen, without editing or making a summary. (*ibid.*, p. 37)

The document cites other worrying statistics. Schools in Northern Ireland spend less per pupil on ICT resources than schools in England. This applies at both primary and post-primary level. What's more, the proportion of computers that are more than four years old is almost twice as high in Northern Ireland as in England.

The DENI document urges the need for improvement in both equipment and training, and it points to raising the level of teacher competence as 'probably the single most important factor in providing the impetus for ICT development in schools'. Teacher training will play its part as well. ICT skills are now among those listed in the profile of competences for student teachers, and funding has been made available for a sustained effort to upgrade ICT skills in the profession generally.

However, such commendable plans for ICT at an official level face a number of awkward realities in many English departments. Most English graduates who join the teaching profession, in Northern Ireland as elsewhere, bring with them an expertise that centres on literature. Their experience of ICT in secondary school may well have been marginal. Certainly their Arts degree at university will have sought to foster an interest in literature rather than technology; ICT is unlikely to have featured prominently in their degree course. Some of them may even be Sarah Laitners.

THE STUDENT TEACHERS

To test the validity of such assumptions and as a beginning in mapping their experience and perceptions, a typical group of fifteen aspiring English teachers had a questionnaire issued to them. These were all English graduates registered on a one-year initial teacher training course (the Postgraduate Certificate in Education, PGCE) at the University of Ulster. The question-naire examined their experience of ICT before embarking on the teacher training year, during the first and second term of that year, and during their first teaching practice period in schools. Interviews were conducted with a number of students and with the university tutor involved in ICT work with the students.

Returns from the questionnaires indicated a limited background in ICT, with four-fifths of students knowing little or very little about ICT when they came on the PGCE course. However, the five students interviewed all had experience of computers for word processing. They admitted to some apprehension about the ICT component of the PGCE course but approached the area in a positive spirit. The course tutor confirmed that most students had little experience of ICT. Even those who started by suggesting they had word-processing skills were found to be relatively weak in this area.

Because of the limited ICT experience of many students, the tutor started the first term with word-processing basics: 'Switching on, seeing the desktop, opening the hard disk, opening ClarisWorks, etc.' Students then embarked on a number of simple tasks – changing the font, putting text in columns, looking at basic desktop publishing. The tutor was aware of his own relatively limited ICT experience: 'I was like the teacher with the A Level group – I was one page ahead of the class.' However, the work was approached in a collaborative spirit, with the expertise of those few students who had an ICT background being called on to help solve problems that arose.

From word processing the class moved to accessing the Internet and using a search engine. These skills established, students were given a task based on the fourth- and fifth-form GCSE syllabus. They were asked to select one poet from the twentieth century and one from the pre-twentieth-century period. They were then required to scan the Internet for information about, and criticism of, the poet, as well as the text of their poems. These, along with relevant images, were to be taken from the Internet and placed in an 'Internet notebook', which was later edited. The culmination of first-term work was to produce a portfolio of materials which would help in the study of the poets in question, and an attractive worksheet based on a selected poem by each poet. This done, each student presented the contents of their portfolio to the rest of the class.

ICT work in the second term was also syllabus-based, this time drawn from the sixth-form A Level English curriculum. Students were asked to think of themselves as members of a small English department. Their task was to provide A Level English resources for the department, drawing on poetry, prose and drama. This work was to be organized in the form of a teacher's pack. This would include a rationale for the work, materials from the Internet and selected strategies for teaching.

This work was found to be successful, with more than half the students indicating that they had developed in their knowledge of ICT a good deal or a great deal since coming on the teacher training course. Student interviews suggested satisfaction that they could now tap into Internet resources for teaching more effectively. There was, however, some uneasiness among students about managing ICT work with pupils in schools. The course tutor looked forward to further development in this and other areas. The use of a computer conferencing system would make it easier for students to share ICT ideas and materials, and increased attention to the pedagogy of ICT work – how materials might best be used with a class in the course of a 40-minute period – would develop student confidence in using ICT with pupils.

For the most part students were warm in their praise of the ICT aspect of the course. For many of them, the depth of English-related material to be found on the Internet came as a revelation. They also developed an awareness of the breadth of material; researching one topic on the Internet threw up other areas which might at another time be of real use. Exploration was also seen as having a creative element, encouraging new thinking about ICT teaching as well as providing resources. Perhaps most important, a beginning was made in the cultivation of self-belief: 'All the lab practice helped to build up my confidence/knowledge in working with computers.' What for many had been unknown territory was beginning to become familiar.

But only beginning. Despite the complimentary remarks regarding progress in ICT in the university, student–teacher confidence regarding ICT use on teaching practice remained a cause for concern. Almost two-thirds of those surveyed felt 'Not very confident' prior to going on their first teaching practice. Much of this apprehension related to the practicalities of using ICT with pupils. 'If you take a class to the ICT room you have to have your objectives and the lesson well focused. You can waste so much time on the Internet.'

As it turned out, apprehension about ICT work during teaching practice proved in many instances unfounded; almost two-thirds of student teachers were given no opportunity to use ICT. It may have been that the host schools believed the student teacher was confronting a sufficient number of challenges and decided to postpone ICT work to ease the teaching burden. Such English departments would deserve commendation for their foresight in protecting the student from negative teaching experiences. However, nothing in the questionnaire returns or the interviews suggests this was the case. It also seems unlikely that so many students would have no opportunity to use ICT if it were being employed in a major way by English departments. As the case studies of schools will later show, not all English departments are happy with their present level of development. Whatever the reason, students feel that English department staff in four-fifths of schools did not encourage them to use ICT.

That said, there are grounds for believing that a distinction can be drawn between staff attitudes to ICT and its resourcing. The findings show that students rate two-thirds of schools as having 'quite good' or 'very good' ICT facilities. It would appear that the opportunity for staff and student teachers to develop ICT expertise exists in terms of equipment. What seems lacking is the expertise and/or the will to use it. Those students who had the opportunity to use ICT in English during teaching practice were involved with word processing. They believed this experience gave pupils the opportunity to feel good about their work when it was presented in a clean, organized copy. Two-thirds of students felt they had learnt 'virtually nothing' about ICT in English during teaching practice. School equipment, they reported, was in some cases very good, but often 'the confidence wasn't there to exploit it to its fullest potential – there wasn't a high degree of expertise among staff'. One student explained how, in his school, 'ICT was frowned upon. The HoD was extremely reluctant – in fact she refused point-blank to use it at all. And there wasn't much enthusiasm or expertise within the department.' Despite this, students hoped to make fuller use of ICT on the second teaching practice. This included plans to set up intranet systems and to make fuller use of CD-Roms and relevant software for teaching Shakespeare and the novel.

The questionnaire revealed a range of areas in which students felt the need for development – everything from accessing the Internet more efficiently to fuller use of PCs rather than Apple Macs. A recurring theme, however, was student concern with expertise in the use of ICT with a class, as distinct from ICT as a resource. There was a belief among most students that the experience of working with pupils in a computing lab needs to be prepared for, to cope with such matters as problems in differentiation. 'Basically, just strategies to spur the pupils on to be more creative – strategies to use in the classroom, how to manage an ICT class – those would be very helpful.' When the questionnaire asked students what advice they would offer a student teacher beginning to use ICT, the emphasis was firmly on the need for preparation. Practical matters predominated: the need to check that machines are working; to have an instructions booklet indicating exactly the steps to be followed; to anticipate problems; to have a back-up lesson for use when the ICT lesson collapses. All of these link to the concern for classroom management skills in the use of ICT.

The tutor listed two matters in particular which require attention if ICT is to realize its potential on the PGCE course: up-to-date and reliable equipment, and strong and continuing technical support. At present both are seen as inadequate. 'And if it's like this for us in training institutions, what in God's name is it like in the schools?' There is also a need for university staff to have the time and support needed to develop their own ICT skills. 'I need maybe months to sit with a careful guide. I don't think the institution or the Department of Education for Northern Ireland [DENI] is fully aware of what they're talking about in these terms.' And the tutor agrees with students on the need for enhanced pedagogical skills. 'You can do this, that, experience this, that. But nobody has explored how it can be done in the classroom. It's about time somebody wrote the text.'

Pedagogy is clearly the issue that emerges with greatest emphasis when student teachers and their tutor are asked their views. For both it raises problems which are not easily resolved. Given the pace of ICT development, few tutors in teacher training institutions have had sustained experience of teaching ICT in English secondary school classrooms. In contrast to other aspects of the curriculum, this is an area where they will not be able to offer students first-hand insights into the problems and possibilities of classroom work. One partial remedy might be for the tutors to locate examples of good practice in schools and base their training on that. Unfortunately, as we have seen, there may not be many English departments where such excellence is on display. This could leave students caught between two unsatisfactory alternatives. In the university, they may encounter little of the practical reality of ICT in the English classroom, because the tutor has not had such experience. In schools, they may find English departments with little enthusiasm for, or expertise in, ICT.

Yet the question persists: why should student teachers feel pedagogical anxiety in terms of ICT and less anxiety regarding such areas as reading, writing, talking and listening? The most obvious distinction between ICT and other areas is that ICT involves the use of hardware and software. If practical confidence in working with computers could be enhanced, pedagogical confidence might follow, but the development of such confidence within a single initial teacher training year presents difficulties. If a candidate for the teacher training course in English were to indicate that he or she knew 'little' or 'very little' about poetry, the novel or writing, tutors might well have doubts about accepting such a candidate. Making up the deficit within the twelve weeks at university would be an impossibility.

Nor would the 24 weeks of school-based experience be likely to contribute significantly. As we've seen, for most student teachers teaching practice offers virtually nothing in terms of development in using ICT. Clearly there is a need for greater co-ordination, if the Department of Education's hopes of developing student teachers in this area are to be realized. The Department has opted for an emphasis on school-based teacher education, with 24 weeks spent in the school and twelve in the university. At present, for two-thirds of students concerned to develop their ICT skills, at least half of their period in schools has been a waste of time.

PRACTISING TEACHERS

What has been reported so far about ICT in English departments has been from the perspective of student teachers. There are a range of reasons why their views and their experience may not reflect the everyday reality of ICT work in schools. It may be that departments believe it important to ground student teachers in more traditional aspects of English teaching first, or that they see ICT work in English as placing excessive demands on student teachers. Whatever the reason, it seemed important to experience first-hand some of the uses to which ICT is put by practising English teachers. What follows are short case studies drawn from three secondary schools in Northern Ireland – two in Belfast, one some 30 miles outside the city. A number of lessons featuring ICT were observed, and twenty-minute interviews conducted with the teacher who taught the lesson and at least one other teacher from the English department. In this way it was hoped to map the contours of ICT in a number of classrooms and allow teachers to reflect on and interpret their experiences of ICT work.

SCHOOL 1

This is an integrated school (Catholics and Protestants, girls and boys) in a rural setting. The Head of Department has seven years' teaching experience. She takes the first lesson, lasting 35 minutes, with fifteen pupils in Year 10. It takes place in a computer lab where there are twenty Apple Mac computers.

Lesson 1

The teacher reminds the class that before Christmas they were working on their personalized stories. They can access that work from the computer they are now seated at. They will be working on these stories today; other ICT work combining elements of English and Maths and focusing on a Ski Trip, is not ready for working on yet. A database will have to be established for this work and they will return to it later. Sheets containing instructions for their story will be coming round, telling them what kind of story it is and how they might write it. 'Now you're going to go into ClarisWorks. Click on word processing and you should be ready to start.'

The sheet distributed to the class has two parts. Part 1 lists six topics for 'creating a personalized story for a six-year-old boy'. The topics include 'The circus comes to town', 'My favourite birthday book', 'A day at the seaside' and 'My favourite pets'. Part 2 tells the pupils to use the personalized story they have created in Part 1 and produce a story-book version for a 3-year-old girl from a different family, for the story corner of the local library. They must think about the names and other words they will include, the size and amount of text, the graphics and the layout.

This hand-out comes from the Council for Curriculum, Examination and Assessment (CCEA) in Northern Ireland. It is headed 'Using IT: Communication Levels 4 & 5'. Its aim is 'to develop and apply [pupils'] knowledge, skills and understanding of IT and use appropriate communication tools for different tasks'. Graphics for the task are taken from a CD-Rom.

As the pupils work, the teacher moves around the room solving technical problems, helping with spelling and curbing those who are talking and distracting others. One boy needs reminding that the story is for a 6-year-old. Another is told to be sure he puts personal details into his story – details relating to the child in question. Virtually all of the pupils are paying attention to their computer and working on the story; at the same time most maintain a steady dialogue with classmates sitting nearby. When the bell sounds the teacher tells the pupils to save their work and that they will come back to it next week. It may even be possible to get a double period then. Pupils are reminded how to save material.

Two girls from the class tell me that they think the boys in the class enjoy computer work more than girls. Both these girls have a computer at home, but in each case it belongs to their dad and is very slow so they don't use it very much. One of the girls says she would prefer to write her story in longhand and then type it in, as she is a very slow typist. She likes the graphics that the task involves. Both say they are doing this story for a real 6-year-old, and it may be that the teacher will let them actually give the story to the child at some future date. The emphasis from pupils and teacher is on the presentation of work rather than its content. To that extent the dominant concern is with the technicalities of ICT rather than the effective communication of ideas.

Lesson 2

A young teacher with three years' experience takes the second lesson. Like the previous group, it is composed of Year 10s and contains fifteen pupils. This teacher has a particular interest in computer work. She tells the pupils that those who weren't here for the last lesson and who aren't familiar with Mailmerge should gather around her. The others should go into the system and 'check where their graphics will go'. Last lesson's absentees are then told how Mailmerge makes it possible to send information to a series of individuals, personalizing each letter, using the database.

This is work based on a CCEA hand-out and linked to the work being done in Lesson 1. The task for this class is drawn from the Ski Trip section (mentioned in the previous lesson) and is delivered through the Maths and English departments working together. It declares that it is supporting English at Key Stage 3 (Years 8–10), and helps pupils '. . . communicate with wider audiences; develop where appropriate and apply their knowledge, understanding and skills of IT to search for, sort and extract meaningful information; develop where appropriate, and apply their knowledge, understanding and skills of IT and use appropriate communication tools for different tasks' (this is taken from the official Programme of Study for English).

The teacher again moves around the room, solving technical problems and pupil questions regarding interpretation of instructions. She reminds those working on the newsletter to 'highlight the title, get some nice colour, get a suitable font into it'. When the bell sounds, the teacher tells the class that it is now lunchtime, they must save their work and tidy up the place before they leave. Gradually, and with some reluctance, the class responds. I talk with one boy, who tells me he likes this kind of work ('It's not as boring as writing'). He's also impressed by Mailmerge; if it wasn't for the computer, he says, he'd have to write 40 letters rather than just one. He hasn't actually written the letter yet – today he's learning how Mailmerge works. The emphasis in the work appears to be on the development of ICT skills rather than on problems of communication or effective use of language.

Teacher interviews

The HoD is aware that staff have 'a long way to go'. In terms of using e-mail or the Internet she herself needs training. She received little preparation for ICT during her teacher training year and there have been many changes since then. The development of ICT in her work has been sporadic, 'Squeezing a lesson in here and in there – the kids knew more than I did.' There has been some in-service training, but most of what she knows has come through her own efforts – taking the computer home, working on it, asking when she encounters problems.

The younger teacher didn't have training on her PGCE: 'It was supposed to be time-tabled but it didn't develop.' But she is interested in ICT and feels able to cope. She's on the IT committee for policy in the school and there are plans to audit the ICT needs of the school. The HoD feels some unhappiness that she must develop ICT skills and understanding in her own time. 'I want to learn the skills – I can't deny the value of ICT as an educational tool. But I do resent the time not being made for it.' The younger teacher says she likes working on the computer at home – enjoys getting better at using it. But she does appreciate that not every staff member might have her interest in ICT.

Both teachers see problems in terms of continuity, with pupils timetabled for just one lesson a week. Difficulties can arise when a pupil falls behind for one reason or another. The example of Mailmerge in the lesson today is cited. Some pupils were familiar with the system, some weren't. 'You're running around doing twenty things', the younger teacher says. 'I sometimes use the lesson before the class to get them focused in advance.' The HoD sees a crowded curriculum as a difficulty, with many areas competing for attention. 'We have to face the problem, do we have drama as a separate subject? Then there's the media component, and the reading, writing, speaking and listening. With so many components, something else would have to fall by the wayside.' One possible answer would be to sacrifice the weekly library period, but both teachers are reluctant to do this, given its importance in promoting reading. The younger teacher thinks there might even be a case for sacrificing the weekly ICT lesson: 'They're getting ICT in Maths and other subjects anyway.'

The teachers value ICT as giving confidence to children who are lacking it. Drafting and editing work is also less of a problem with ICT – amending text is easier and more flexible, and pupils don't want their work to be finalized until it is right. ICT is not seen as particularly appropriate for the GCSE class – they're not very independent on the computer 'so it would be a waste of time'. In addition, where literature is being studied, the pressure to cover the curriculum doesn't permit much ICT work. Both teachers are keen that ICT work is not just busy work or meaningless, with the teacher engaging in it purely so it can be said that ICT work has happened with an English class. 'If you go up and say "Write out a poem, add colour", you're just trying to push IT. But with these projects (the personalized story, the Ski Trip) they are structured, there's a goal at the end. They must consider what's the best way to present the information. And you know that this work should be finished inside a particular time, and that it's at a particular level. You could develop your own work, but this way it's recognized and you know you're doing the right thing.'

The younger teacher believes that ICT engages the pupils more than some other areas of the English curriculum. She sees it as linking to areas more relevant than literature – letters, newspaper articles, etc. The HoD believes ICT highlights the importance of presentation. 'With a slap-dash child, you say "Let's go to the IT suite" – and suddenly they're more careful regarding spelling and punctuation. They hate having anything printed up that's not perfect.' The HoD highlights two things: 'Money and time.' There is a need for money to train staff, with teaching cover provided, and time so that they're not doing it all in a lunch hour or during a department meeting. The younger teacher agrees. She feels that older teachers are now more positive towards ICT. If the Internet were up and running this would help further, with pupils able to communicate with others. The HoD notes that the Internet is an area in which she needs training, in common with many other teachers. 'We need some intensive training, and then time to practise and consolidate what we've learned.'

The positive attitude of the teachers towards ICT is impressive. Even with a crowded English curriculum, they have little doubt that ICT has a valuable contribution to make to English. There may be concern about other aspects of their work, but their concern is to use ICT more effectively rather than question its use. Unusually, perhaps, they have no complaints about equipment. 'We're in a unique position', the HoD says, 'we're so well equipped. We have regular access to computers – we've both one at home, we can use them all the time. Printers are the only thing we lack.' The fact that the school is still waiting for the Internet to be established is not seen as a major problem. This may be because of the many other aspects of ICT which require training. The problem as they see it is how to cope with the riches presently available.

Both teachers place emphasis on the need for training. The concern is to develop expertise, and there is a willingness if necessary to use evenings or other leisure time to develop that expertise. While student teachers emphasize the need for instruction in pedagogy, these teachers stress the need for technical know-how. At the same time, both teachers are appreciative of ready-made classroom materials. They are willing to follow the tasks supplied by the CCEA, which provide aims and levels and outline step-by-step what to do with the children. There is less concern to analyse or debate the place of ICT within English.

This is hardly surprising given that ICT is a new field for most teachers. In such circumstances it is natural to seek the reassurance that official sanction provides. The tasks involved in the lessons, with their emphasis on audience and vocabulary, and the relationship between text and image, all relate clearly to the prescribed English curriculum. However, the list of topics for the personalized story – for example, 'A Day at the Seaside' – has an old-fashioned flavour. Such topics for writing pre-date ICT by at least 30 years. This contrasts with the more open thinking of the student teachers, who seemed aware of the new notions of literacy which ICT offers. For example, when they drew materials from the Internet to support more traditional aspects of the English course, they took the opportunity to support print material with images – of writers, landscapes and themes. They are also aware that the communication element of ICT, involving such things as e-mail and computer conferencing, makes unique demands on the written word not available through more traditional written work. Beyond this, ICT draws us into the world of multi-media communication, where the written word may be for speaking rather than reading, or for supporting visual communication, or related to music and other sound effects. It is this vision of literacy which appears as yet underdeveloped in some classrooms.

In fact, if we look at the traditional tasks given without reference to new literacies, pupils appear to be embarking on these 'creative' tasks with no preparation in terms of memories, shared emotions, note-taking, observation – none of the things that go into creative writing in the real world. Despite the linkage at an official level, concern with mastery of ICT procedures may be overshadowing concern with the kind of personal growth that writing makes possible.

SCHOOL 2

This is a Protestant all-boys secondary school in inner-city North Belfast. The school has a pupil population of over 1,000, with some 70 teachers. Most of the boys at 11 years of age would either have been unsuccessful in, or not sat, the Transfer Examination (the examination used to select the top 30 per cent of pupils who go on to the more academic grammar school). The English Department Head has been teaching for twenty years.

The lesson

The work in the computer lab took place on a Friday afternoon. It emerged that this was not in fact a formal English period but a computer club session, organized and supervised by two members of the English department. It was attended by some 30 Year 8 and 9 boys, with an addition of two Year 11 boys who were completing some work for Maths. There were twenty computers in the room, with most boys having a machine each. Two teachers – one with four years' experience, one in her first year teaching – supervised the work.

The teachers had spent the first term allowing the boys to become familiar with the basic workings of the machines. This term they are starting on a series of bronze, silver and gold certificates (devised by one of the teachers). The level reached is decided by the number of tasks completed – 8 for a bronze, 10 for a silver, 15 for a gold. Tasks include business cards, advertisements, posters, newspapers, joke books and greeting cards. One of the teachers tells the pupils to settle at their machines; she will come around and see how they are getting on. She reminds them of the various tasks involved in going for a certificate.

The boys are engaged in their work and occasionally confer together. The two teachers move around encouraging the pupils, asking them about what they are doing, giving solutions where technical difficulties arise. One boy is working on a menu, he says. He has the icons for the top of the menu in place (chosen for appearance rather than meaning – they include one for a religious document, one for a holiday, one for business) but he has still to decide what his menu will be concerned with. There are a number of certificates for Rangers or Liverpool Football Club. Flags of various kinds are particularly popular. One boy is busy creating shapes of different colours. After some thought, he writes a title for his creation. Another has a picture of a bearded man, which he has taken from a library of such figures. He has added an explosion of light over the head and written in 'Sinn Fein'. Only one boy has developed written work. He has created a story about a 'Queen Anne of Carrickfergus.' His teacher encourages him in this and helps him with some spellings. Two Year 11 boys are also present. One is typing up a letter for work experience, the other creating a sheet of stars for a science project. They complete their work and leave. Throughout, the teachers move around the room, encouraging and guiding and keeping order with a very light touch. The sense that this is a voluntary activity is clear.

Teacher interviews

The two young teachers note that they received little ICT instruction during teacher training, but believe they have a level of competence that will sustain them. In contrast the HoD considers his ICT knowledge inadequate, but feels he is learning from younger teachers coming into the department. He has recently been at an in-service day which introduced him to e-mail and the Internet, but his skills remain limited: 'I'm walking on quicksand.'

The major problem for the two young teachers is the resourcing of ICT. Their computer club takes place in the ICT lab, but this is not available to them on a regular basis. And even if it were, there would not be enough computers. In addition, the pupils in Year 10 and beyond do not have very good keyboard skills. They would be in a state of high excitement and hard to control if brought up to the lab. There is also the need to have a technician on hand to attend to machines when they malfunction, as they often do. The HoD says he is tired of hearing talk of a computer in every room. He'd like to see the reality of such things.

The teachers believe ICT is particularly helpful for the development of writing. The Internet is seen as having 'so many resources on it', it would also be helpful for developing reading. ICT work has the advantage of matching with the pupils' interests, the teachers believe. 'They're used to visual technology all the time. You can almost con them into reading sometimes with computers.' The HoD believes ICT is particularly helpful for working with the non-academic pupil. When such a pupil puts his coursework onto the computer, he feels positive about it. 'Essays which emerge as typed text give them a buzz.'

The two teachers see ICT as a support to the English curriculum. 'If it's going to get them to read and write, it's a good thing in some ways. But it does seem a bit faddish, and it's not possible all the time.' To some extent it might even draw pupils away from central concerns of English, but that would be a passing phase. 'Once the novelty of the computer would wear off, you can draw them back to books.' The HoD feels 'tentatively excited'. He works with a wide range of ability and finds that ICT has an attraction and a motivation for all levels of ability. Many of the pupils, even in relatively deprived homes, now have a PC; sometimes they are the ones who establish the link of their work with ICT. To some extent education is following what is happening in society in terms of ICT, rather than leading.

The two younger teachers feel the need for training in 'how to use ICT effectively and meaningfully in English'. Any training would have to be realistic and take into account the level of ability and the social skills of the pupils involved. If it were possible to observe examples of good practice in action – an actual ICT lesson in progress, the management of the work – that would be helpful. 'I don't even know if I'm using the best format.' The HoD urges the need for 'a systematic proactive training scheme for all my teachers, and a follow-up at least once a term. And the hardware resources.' He stresses the willingness of teachers to take such training, even in their own time. 'I need expertise, updated courses – I'd be happy to learn at night. And my staff would.'

The session observed and the conversation with the teachers and the HoD suggest that ICT is at an early stage of development within English classes here. The availability of computers is a major difficulty – it is unusual, I am told, for an English classroom to have even one computer in the room. The computer suite appears to be heavily booked for other uses, but there is also an unwillingness to bring classes to it for fear of over-excitement and disruption.

There is some divergence of experience and opinion between the two teachers and the HoD. The teachers have had little training but feel comfortable with what they have; the HoD has had little training but is keen to develop. The teachers tend to emphasize the motivating power of ICT; it is seen as something of a lure, which then can lead to books and other aspects of the curriculum. The HoD talks in terms of a closer integration between English and ICT. Pupils' written work is better and pupils find resources of relevance to their literature course by dipping into the Internet in their own time. The importance attached to the computer club and the willingness with which the pupils work at it suggests a focus on the technology rather than the aims of the English curriculum. As the CCEA materials provided a legitimizing structure for the work in the first school, so the bronze/silver/gold certificates provide a direction for the work the pupils are following. However, while the first school had pupils actively engaged in following the stages of the CCEA work, the pupils here have, in many instances, scarcely begun the work that will lead to a certificate. For the most part, the ICT work is at the level of play – flags, designs and cartoon figures.

SCHOOL 3

This school is the sister school of the boys' school described above. It has a pupil population of over 1,000 girls and a staff of 70 teachers. The pupils come from inner-city areas of North Belfast and most would have failed or not sat the Transfer Examination.

The lesson

The lesson takes place in a computer lab containing 25 computers. The class consists of thirty Year 8 girls and the lesson lasts 60 minutes. While the teacher for this lesson is an English teacher, she does not take this particular class for English. They have this double period in the lab with her once a week, and she admits to some difficulty in adjusting the work to fit with what pupils are doing during the rest of the week.

The teacher calls for attention and reads out the names of a number of girls. Girls who are 'well ahead' in their work are then asked to give their computer up to one of those named and share at another work station. The 'well-ahead' girls show signs of not being totally happy with this arrangement.

The class is asked to start with ten minutes' work on 'Mavis Beacon'. This is a typing tutorial program, where pupils are asked to type the letters listed, a fanfare sounds when they complete the task successfully and they move to the next stage. The girls work quietly, chatting to each other occasionally. The teacher moves around the room seeing that they are settled, checking if people are having difficulties and are on-task. The Mavis Beacon task completed, the pupils move to a booklet produced by the CCEA. This contains activities under a range of headings: for example, Myself, Career Leaflet, Personalized Story, Newspaper Review and Car-Boot Sale. The level for each of these pieces of work is stipulated. When they have completed a set number of tasks, pupils will receive a Certificate of Competence.

The teacher calls the class to attention and announces that those girls with individual access to a computer should be submitting a completed copy of 'Myself' to her. 'There are still a lot of girls [who] have to insert a graphic onto that piece. Find your folder and find what you still have to do.' A number of instruction manuals circulate which advise on how to complete a number of computer procedures. Pupils consult the booklet occasionally but more often turn to the teacher when they encounter a technical problem. A girl brings up her work, is complimented and her work put in a folder.

The teacher works with pupils in turn. She advises a pupil on how to put her graphic at a particular point in relation to text. She explains to another girl how to print, and advises another who has finished to 'go into the spelling game today'. With the lesson two-thirds completed, the teacher makes an announcement: 'Anybody else who is not clear how to insert a graphic on their work, I will demonstrate now on Leanne's computer. If you're not sure about it, take a pencil with you to take notes.'

Some of the girls have finished and go into programs where they can type their name and then make it assume different shapes and colours. The teacher continues to check how many people have submitted a 'Myself' document. This typically consist of the girl's name, that of her parents, brothers and sister, where she lives, etc. Some of these are up to 500 words in length.

With ten minutes remaining, the teacher calls those who are finished to a table in the centre of the room. She passes round some booklets and the girls look through these. The teacher explains that 'Myself' was for Level Three, and Level Four if you put a graphic in it. The next piece – for Levels Four and Five – is a move up. 'Find the Little Theatre section. Now, what I want you to do in the remaining seven minutes is go back to your desks, read through the tasks, think about what you are going to do – sketch a quick plan of the poster, maybe. Are you going to use Clip Art, or go to ClarisWorks – plan and think about what you may be going to do. But take the booklet and read the task now.' With a few minutes remaining, the teacher again calls for the class's attention: 'Girls working on computers still – save what you're doing and log off. Julie will collect the Introduction to IT booklets, Leanne will collect the Pupils booklet. Please remain seated.'

Good order and commitment to the task is evident throughout the lesson. The focus of the work is clear, with pupils knowing just what they have to do, with help available if they run into problems. There is no sense of time-wasting or pupils merely amusing themselves. The lesson has an emphasis on the written word rather than graphics – the graphics are an extra after the 'Myself' written portrait has been produced. The graphics do attract the children, as is evidenced in their moving to this kind of work when they have completed the required task, but they are aware that producing the written work is what counts. However, where pupils are looking for assistance from the teacher, it invariably is in connection with a technical problem, rather than an attempt to cope with a problem of expression. To that extent, the technology is what is taking the pupils' attention rather than the writing task.

Teacher interview
This was conducted with the Head of Department, who has nine years' teaching experience, and the teacher who took the class, who has three.

The teacher had very little ICT training in her PGCE year. However, she took a word-processing/databases/spreadsheet summer course, prior to her first year of teaching. This year she is the English department's ICT representative. During the Christmas holidays she took a one-day course in HTML, and will be going on a five-day ICT course in the near future. 'There seems to be plenty of opportunities and I am very willing to be involved.' The HoD has developed her level of expertise in her own time and through working with the pupils. She feels comfortable with her level of knowledge and skills.

For the teacher, one of the major problems is in terms of management. 'Pupils are motivated and enjoy ICT lessons. But they should get more help. I have a class of 30 pupils and there aren't 30 computers in the room. Given this, the question is, how can the tasks be best managed – whether by dividing the class or having two teachers working with the one class.' For the HoD, the main problem lies with resources. 'Money. So we can actually get into the machines. We could have wonderful ideas for *Romeo and Juliet* – for using Quicktime – but if we come down and find a room is not available, it's no use. There's a need for more machines, more often. The link between hardware and management is obvious.'

The teacher feels that writing is the most useful area for ICT within English. 'I think it reinforces the need for drafting and the ease with which that can be done. The pupils are willing, they see how easy it is and they take pride in their work.' The Internet is seen as less valuable at present. Some groups of girls have been sent to the library with a specific list of sites to check out. The librarian has been able to supervise them, and a check made of sites visited. However, not all pupils would always have the skill to evaluate and decide what was worthwhile or true. 'We're trying to set up an intranet site, and from a teacher's point of view feel secure that pupils aren't working off-task.'

The HoD stresses the worth of ICT for reading development. 'My worry is, coming into the new millennium, we'll have to teach children new sets of reading skills with the Internet, etc. There are search strategies, for example, that they need to be sat down and taught – that kind of thing doesn't come naturally. And they need to be taught to discriminate in what they read and use – for example, if pupils are told to gather materials on the First World War, they tend to go into the Internet and take everything out. There isn't sufficient interaction with the text.'

The teacher feels the value of ICT lies in the opportunities it creates. An example cited is the Year 9s, who now are creating their own web pages and forging links with feeder primary schools, finding ways of communicating with those schools. The fact that they were part of the previous Year 8 ICT programme has made a great deal of difference. The HoD believes that the possibilities of wider audiences for written work are of vital significance. 'The pupils here are writing for Primary 7s – and those Primary 7s are going to actually read it. It's no longer a paper exercise.' At the same time she stressed the fact that at Year 11/Year 12 level, in terms of literature, there was little time left for ICT after the regular course had been 'ploughed through'.

Even though the lesson observed had used ready-made CCEA work for ICT in English, both the teacher and the HoD resist the notion of such processed materials. The teacher said: 'The course I'm going to next week, I've been asked to bring the English Programme of Study. I think that means they're going to look for opportunities where ICT can be implemented, rather than concentrate on developing teacher skills.' The HoD said: 'I don't think you need to be trained in how to implement. You are always thinking of ways to deliver the curriculum. You need to be made aware of what the machines can do. It's a waste of time, if you're doing *Macbeth* and you go on a course and they say, "Here are the nice things you could do with *Macbeth*."'

Both teachers believe that those who are setting policy for ICT within English should be aware of the practical difficulties involved for the teacher. The teacher wonders how a DENI person would cope with the demands of a Year 8 class, last two periods on a Monday: 'I'd like to see him/her deal with all the pupils so demanding and all the technical problems.' The HoD feels that it is not always appreciated how little ICT background pupils coming from primary school have, nor the time it takes to perform ICT tasks, with all of the pressures to do other things within the English curriculum. 'If they can't provide an increase in hardware, an increase in technical support would be nice – someone continually available to cope with problems.'

Once again training has been limited, but both teachers feel confident that they can cope with what is required. Their concerns centre on resources, the implications these have for the kind of work they can embark on and the problems of classroom management they must constantly confront. There is the usual awareness of the benefits that the computer can offer to the drafting of work, but the HoD's awareness of the demands on reading made by the Internet offers a new perspective. The suggestion is that besides offering a support for English, ICT creates new kinds of literacy tasks.

A constant theme with these two teachers is the need for attention to the reality of things. The tasks the pupils are set – linking with Primary 7 pupils – should be real tasks, making real demands. Likewise, the Department of Education needs to consider the reality of classroom management with limited resources, when they are making policy or producing materials.

There is also a strong awareness of the importance of teachers using ICT to achieve their aims and objectives for English work, rather than being given ready-made tips on using ICT with specific texts. There is a belief that teachers know best in these matters and should be helped, through developing their skills, to construct their own links between the English curriculum and ICT.

CONCLUSION

This brief survey of the state of ICT in English at pre-service and in-service level provides grounds for optimism. At both university- and school-level there is a drive to establish ICT within the student teacher/teacher's repertoire of skills. The PGCE course is making increased provision for ICT instruction; the three English departments are positive in their attitude to the use of ICT and are using it in a variety of forms with their pupils. Student teachers and teachers are concerned to develop their ICT skills and are prepared to give of their leisure time to do so.

Supporting much of this teacher goodwill is an awareness that ICT is viewed positively by pupils, its motivating force particularly evident with the less academic. (Goodwyn *et al.*, 1997, also found positive attitudes, for similar reasons, among teachers in England.) This contribution of ICT to the development of weaker pupils has particular significance for Northern Ireland, where some 70 per cent of pupils attend less academic secondary schools. While most grammar school pupils have the expectation of examination success, this is less evident among secondary school pupils, who may be in greater need of alternative motivation. ICT can and does provide this: even when attendance at an ICT session was optional, pupils willingly attended.

There are also signs that pupils develop a stronger sense of ownership with ICT. They take a pride in the appearance of their work, sometimes going to considerable pains to bring it to the required level. This may relate to the fact that many pupils feel a confidence in working with images which they don't feel in more traditional work. ICT allows them the opportunity to combine the visual and the verbal, one enhancing the other. In such circumstances, the completed work resembles more closely the kind of media text – whether electronic or print – which pupils are likely to encounter in the outside world. On the other hand, it may simply be that ICT allows them to by-pass the problems of poor handwriting and grubby presentation which traditionally bedevil the weaker pupil. Whatever the reason, pupils appear to have a sense of fuller control over their work.

Some teachers seem aware of the new possibilites for literacy which ICT offers. While the Internet confronts them with problems in terms of undesirable sites and focus on the task in hand, it also offers positive challenges. The resources of the Internet invite the construction of newspaper articles, brochures, advertisements, etc. To respond successfully to that invitation calls for new kinds of literacy skills: the ability to scan huge areas of information; select in view of a particular audience; communicate with a particular audience; interact with materials in the light of individual aims. Thus the responsibility for successful learning passes to pupils, and they show signs of being willing to shoulder it. Work of this nature also allows pupils a greater say in content. This was seen in the case of School 2, where pupils selected their own menu, flag, logo, etc. for working on. The task of the teacher in such situations must be to give direction and encouragement to pupils, pointing them to tasks that stretch their thought and understanding. The attendant possibilities for effective differentiation in task and outcome are obvious.

Student teachers and practising teachers show a concern to develop their own skills and understanding of ICT. Students are particularly anxious to develop in terms of classroom management and discipline. They are eager to know how pupils can be brought to the computer lab without over-excitement, how in practical terms a teacher can support a class of twenty or more in their work. With different emphases, teachers share these concerns. Some stress the importance of structure in ICT work and welcome 'packaged' materials; these give them ready-made organization and a reassurance that the work meets with official approval. Others emphasize the need for technical know-how and resist the prospect of having classroom work on specific areas managed for them.

One answer for the concerns of both groups might be examples of excellence: a successful English teacher using ICT, whether in the form of a demonstration lesson to which teachers were invited or a demonstration lesson on video-tape with accompanying commentary and discussion points. Teachers could then decide whether to follow the model closely or loosely, depending on their needs.

This model of teachers helping each other could be paralleled in more collaborative work between teacher and pupils in the classroom. This sense of joint enterprise was apparent in the student teacher work at university. The tutor accepted the existence of areas where students had greater expertise and used this expertise to help move the whole group forward. Given the prevalence of computers in homes and the expertise of some pupils with software and hardware, classrooms might use informal expertise as a planned resource.

It is also worth noting that the university ICT programme firmly links the known to the unknown, the familiar to the less familiar. By concentrating on those areas of the curriculum which have clear and accepted demarcation lines – GCSE and A Level – the university tutor encourages students to develop new ICT skills, confident in the knowledge that these relate to areas of work valued by teachers and pupils. English teachers share this concern to root ICT work firmly in their subject. Some do so by using materials that have the *imprimatur* of the CCEA, indicating specific tasks and the levels which these tasks will offer. Others are concerned to ensure that ICT work grows out of needs in the English curriculum, with ICT playing a supporting and renewing role within English rather than a dominant and distracting one.

This last is of central importance. For a number of reasons, much of the work considered in this study emphasized mastery of computer procedures – how to include graphics, how to save material, where to place an icon. This is to an extent to be expected, since computers are complex machines. The attendant danger, however, is that technical facility rather than English skills and understanding will be given priority. Because the technology can be so dazzling, care must be taken that it does not overshadow those things valued by all English teachers. As one HoD pointed out, the needs of the English curriculum should first be addressed and then how ICT can meet some of those needs. Put another way: ICT must be servant to English, not its master.

Chapter 4

ICT in English:
The Australian Perspective

VAUGHAN PRAIN AND LES LYONS

INTRODUCTION

English teachers in Australia are using information and communication technologies in diverse ways to enhance learning in this subject. In this chapter we want to focus mainly on two case studies of teacher practices that indicate some current and future opportunities and challenges in applying these technologies to teaching secondary English. However, to provide a context within which to consider these practices we first review some current issues raised by recent commentators. These include questions of current unevenness of classroom practices in different settings, and the need to develop adequate models of effective literacy learning in and through the new technologies (Snyder, 1997; Johnson-Eilola, 1997; Kress, 1997; Morgan, 1997; Smith and Curtin, 1997).

While there is a growing recognition that the shift from print to digital technologies necessitates redefinition of the nature of literacy or literacies as well as new teaching methods, what might count as effective learning of literacies in the information age remains problematic. Reviewing national and state policy documents Lankshear, Bigum et al. (1997, p. 15) noted that, while there is much advocacy of getting teachers 'up to speed' in using the new technologies, there is very little policy that deals directly with 'electronic literacy', its nature, or the specific practices that might ensure students become electronically literate. In their study they proposed that this literacy should be defined as having three dimensions: the 'operational' (knowing how to use the technologies), the 'cultural' (understanding the contexts of appropriate use) and the 'critical' (being able to make judgements about the skills, values, beliefs, practices and effects associated with this use). However, they argued that their study of policy and classroom practices indicated that the critical aspect is 'underdeveloped' (p. 16). They also noted that national policy is characterized by lack of dialogue between policy groups in the areas of literacy and technology, and that increased collaboration is needed to create the necessary space to formulate coherent policy for classroom practices.

Other recent research studies have focused on further challenges for effective literacy learning in the information age. Cumming *et al.* (1998, pp. 9–10) in a two-year study of nearly 1,500 secondary students noted that increasingly 'students are expected to use various literacy modes of reading, writing, speaking, listening, viewing and critical thinking in dynamically networked ways' (p. 9), thus engaging in multiple literacies, and yet there is a lack of 'explicit attention' by teachers to developing these co-ordinated skills. Lankshear, Bigum *et al.* (1997, Vol. 1, p. 17) have also pointed out that these skills are now applied to different technologies, including ones that are text-based, such as word processing and desktop publishing, information-based, such as spreadsheets and databases, programming-based, such as LOGO, and games-based, such as Carmen Sandiego.

A further challenge for literacy education, noted by Lankshear, Gee *et al.* (1997), is the continuing gap between teacher and student knowledge and values in using these technologies. These writers, like Sefton-Green (1998), Smith and Curtin (1997) and others, have observed that there is often a striking mismatch between the sophisticated technological understandings and skills students have acquired outside the classroom, and the official and 'domesticated' uses of new technologies proposed for learning the curriculum. However, this student knowledge can also be viewed as an important resource in the development of understanding how to use the new technologies effectively. Lankshear, Gee *et al.* (1997) also note, drawing on Bigum and Green (1992), that electronic literacy now encompasses a range of complex relations between literacy and technology. Technology can be seen as a range of resources for teaching literacy as well as understood as a form of literacy in itself. Equally, literacy can be understood as a form of technology, as a set of tools or practices for achieving diverse ends, and as necessary for using technology, such as reading instructions or using a computer effectively. Lankshear, Gee *et al.* (1997, p. 141) argue that 'technological literacies' should be defined as social practices in which texts are 'constructed, transmitted, received, modified, shared (and otherwise engaged) within processes which are digitised electronically'. In this view, students are electronically literate when they can process words, sounds and images, use or evaluate e-mail and Web information or communication, and can also play or manipulate various electronic games or devices such as joysticks or cursors.

Supporting this general view Burbules (1997a, 1997b) argued that students also need to develop new critical skills in using electronic technologies. They need to go beyond the current skill of checking the credibility of writers or designers in terms of the expertise, impartiality or coherence of what is offered, of distinguishing between information and knowledge. Further, students need to understand the design features of the technologies they are using. For example, they need to understand the role and effects of links in websites, that these links, far from acting as neutral organizers of information, dramatically affect the nature and purposes for reading as well as the meaning and significance of what is linked. While acknowledging that these new capabilities may be understood partly in terms of traditional versions of critical literacy, they also 'involve elements that are distinctive to the digital environment' (1997b, pp. 117–18), with its seductiveness, overwhelming volume of content and speed of delivery. By implication, teachers will also need to understand the design features of each new technology they use for teaching and learning if they are to maximize learning possibilities and avoid pitfalls.

The foregoing points also raise the general issue of which teaching approaches and learning contexts or environments will work best to achieve this literacy. Lankshear, Bigum *et al.* (1997, Vol. 1, p. 18) and others assert that teaching and learning practices that emphasize 'apprenticeship, guided participation and participatory appropriation' with a strong focus on 'authentic or "real life" learning contexts' are likely to succeed. From this perspective, classroom practices should parallel and overlap with the ways new technologies meet and are continually adapted to real economic, civic, personal, cultural and recreational purposes outside the school. In this view, such an agenda means that the English curriculum cannot simply pursue past goals, merely incorporating the technologies as add-on resources, but needs to acknowledge the ways technological practices and capacities are changing significantly what counts as literacy and how this literacy might be learnt.

Tasks and projects in school must match even more closely usage beyond the classroom. At the same time, we do not want to offer students apprenticeships in 'inferior versions of social practices' (Lankshear, Bigum *et al.*, 1997, Vol. 2, p. 74). We want our students to succeed in a networked world, but we do not want to endorse this world's inequities, some of which the new technologies have exacerbated.

Taking this very brief overview of issues into account we would like to focus now on two case studies of the use of information technologies to learning secondary English in Australia. Our intention is not to offer these case studies as exemplary evidence of advanced practices, or as typical or even exceptional work in Australian secondary schools. Rather, each case study reports on ways in which teachers and students in particular curriculum contexts are using the technologies, as well as on their understandings of, and attitude towards, these practices. We believe that these case studies can provide useful insights for other teachers into possible models for planning and implementing strategies to use these technologies for teaching and learning.

ICT IN ENGLISH IN PRACTICE

Our first case study reports on a unit of work on electronic writing with two classes of Year 9 students (14-year-olds) in a private school, Gold Independent College. This was a collaborative project between a teacher-educator in educational technology and two English teachers. The school has a strong academic orientation in the curriculum but limited new technology resources.

There is no computer laboratory, and few of the teachers have their own school computer or much experience with using information and communication technologies.

We were working with two mixed-ability classes, 49 students in total. They were a fairly typical bunch: some bright and enthusiastic who would run ahead of their peers and teacher whenever the opportunity arose, the majority who set the general pace for the classes, some who did only what was demanded of them, several who were reluctant to speak or put pen to paper for fear of showing just how weak their command of language and writing was, and a couple whose goal appeared to be open resistance to all that formal schooling entailed. They had all spent the first half-year working through the prescribed curriculum: a novel, short story, film study, a couple of television studies, newspaper studies and plenty of opportunities to express ideas and responses in different media and formats. Audience was a recurring theme, and for many tasks no one was permitted to write a piece until a precise profile of the intended audience had been produced. A key requirement was that the audience had to change for each piece of writing. For some, the preparation of a clear audience description and a purpose were often more difficult tasks than the written piece to follow, particularly for those whose social contact was limited to peers and parents. 'Why can't I just write like we used to?' became the frequently asked question when the frustration surfaced, as it so frequently does with the emotional roller coaster ride this age group experiences. While English teachers are familiar with the requirement that students understand and meet audience needs in traditional print texts, the new technologies pose new challenges in meeting these needs.

For most activities the audience was largely imaginary, with peers and teachers offering guiding comments on what was appropriate for vocabulary, structure and style. As in most classes the teacher made the final decision on how well the piece matched the proposed audience and stated purpose. After two terms, audience and purpose were becoming more than abstract concepts. The real-world models of writing (including pictures, film and television) were recognized as being quite different for different audiences. Subtle distinctions were being identified and their purposes considered. The keen members of the classes were taking many of these on board and exploring their use in their own writing efforts, albeit rather crudely. Individual writing styles had started to emerge for some, but these often disappeared before the teacher had time to encourage further exploration and development, much to the disappointment of the teachers.

All this was intended to prepare students for an extended activity of electronic 'writing', undertaken in a university teacher education computer laboratory for a two-and-a-half-hour block each fortnight over the next two terms, nine laboratory working sessions for each class. Each class was to take turns using the laboratory for the fixed time each week. Under the general circumstances existing in most schools a project like this would probably not be contemplated by English teachers. The prevailing general lack of computing expertise among secondary teachers, and English teachers in particular, poses what is often perceived as an insurmountable hurdle when school administrators seek to encourage more 'across the curriculum' computer activity. Neither English teacher of these classes had any experience with computers in teaching and neither had any knowledge of what it was like to work with a class in a networked laboratory. This was a school without a laboratory so these issues had not arisen in the development of the school programme and the English curriculum in particular.

In this instance, the perceptual hurdle was not a consideration because the project was instigated by an outsider with computing expertise and an available computer laboratory. To ensure that the project was seen as an integral element in the year's English programme, planning commenced at the end of the previous year when the new course outline was being prepared. The computing teacher was involved in the course development discussions. It was proposed that a range of appropriate preparatory 'writing' exercises be included in the normal first half-year. These posed no particular problems as they fell well within the Government's English Framework guidelines.

It was agreed that the students were to be given no information about the project until the commencement of the third term. A letter to parents seeking their permission for participation in an ongoing off-site English project for two terms distributed at term's end said only that the students would be working with computers. All parents gave permission.

At the commencement of the new term the English teachers presented their classes with a general outline of the project. They would be working in pairs. Pairs were chosen rather than groups because each student gets regular access to the computer, and, based on past experience, pairs have been successful. The pairs had to have teacher approval. The task for each pair was the production of an electronic book on a computer. The book was to be written for a particular audience, a nominated child from a Year 2 class of 7-year-olds. A 'buddy' programme had been agreed to which saw the Year 9 students in each pair rostered to spend some short periods of time with the chosen 'audience' each week throughout the third term. During this time, the older students read stories to the younger, listened to reading, helped with the writing of stories, found out what the child's interests were and sought detail on what they would like a book to be about. Back in their English classrooms the pairs had to compare notes and compile an audience description and agree upon a topic, a purpose and a loose idea for the proposed narrative for their 'ten-page' electronic book. This posed a problem for a couple of pairs as their intended readers gave different topics and/or different content each time they met. As was anticipated, the range of interests ensured that no two pairs of writers shared the same topic.

The students had not met the person with whom they would be working in the laboratory, nor did they have knowledge of what equipment was available in the computer laboratory or what the software would permit them to do. This was a deliberate strategy to encourage the students to plan first, and then produce, with the computer being seen as the tool or means for realizing previously established outcomes rather than the outcomes being decided by what the computer makes possible. It had been agreed that the planning had to be a narrative on paper, in basic storyboard format, and vetted by the English teacher and the collaborating primary school teacher before the classes were to be granted access to the computer laboratory.

The teachers had also been given little detail of what was available. This wasn't deliberate; they just hadn't thought this information was of any value to them or the students. As it turned out this proved to be an advantage because the students who were regular computer users sought the technical information throughout the planning phase. The vetting phase made obvious the influence the range of students' prior knowledge of computer games, animation and the general capabilities of multi-media software had on the ways that topics were planned. Provision for the possible inclusion of animation, sound effects and 'computer talking' were very common among the boys' contributions. The girls, by contrast, generally stuck to a book-like format consisting of a relatively linear narrative of pictures and text. Even those who were experienced computer users appeared to shy away from planning for the possible inclusion of any computer gimmickry. The girls' planned books were, without exception, text-dominated with computer-created pictures to illustrate the story.

In the laboratory the students were allocated a permanent machine for each pair, introduced to the software, initially just the word-processing and colour-painting environments with card or page links and some effects. No experimenting time was offered, as one of the goals was to see how comfortable the students were with mastering the software as the book was being produced. The students were advised that they had a tight schedule and that the purpose of the exercise was to use the time fully to complete the book with one person on the machine and the other acting as director or 'critical friend' and exchanging roles after fifteen minutes. All aspects of this were in the hands of the computing teacher.

The two English teachers did not participate in the early sessions. They stated that they had felt 'awkward', 'out of their depth', 'in the way', and 'useless because I have no idea what they are doing', soon after the students had commenced working on the machines. Both female teachers each had more than twenty years' teaching experience, and had volunteered to participate. Their concerns about their knowledge-base changed significantly from session three when many pairs had some quite substantial work to show. There was a general expectation that the teachers would check work in progress and comment on it in the traditional way. The enthusiasm shown by the students and their willingness to show what had been accomplished and how it had been done overcame the reluctance shown by both teachers, allowing them to engage in the follow-up discussions and planning back in the classroom.

By the end of the fifth session most writing pairs had completed the core narrative, consisting of cards with text and the accompanying outline illustrations, all markedly similar and based largely on the styles of the books being read to their target child in the 'buddies' programme. They were then introduced to a range of options that offered the potential for extending the book by using other dimensions of communication offered by the computer: animation, speak text, sound effects, real audio. They were to select and explore the application of one of the options in a variety of ways. The original storyline narrative was not to be changed and the additions were to be a natural part of the story. All of the options were made as transparent as possible, including a variety of animation options where the scripts had been prepared in advance for cutting, pasting and minor substitution.

It was during the introduction of the options offered by the computer software that a transformation in story presentation occurred. Where the word processing and picture-drawing were relatively private pairs activities (although individual efforts won much praise from peers and teachers), it was the exploration of the simple animation sequences that completely changed the working relationships, both within the laboratory, and back in the classrooms during planning. Experts emerged from among the students for the application of particular techniques. These became consultants to many other pairs who wanted to try something similar. Individual efforts were closely examined for style and effect as the pairs attempted to decide what might work in their own production. At times the computer lab appeared to be more a series of mêlées than a constructive working and learning environment. However, this apparent confusion appeared to contribute to considerable discussion about the value of many proposed additions in terms of what would be suitable for the target audience. Much of the final decision-making occurred after discussion with the English teachers, who were by now regular participants in the laboratory sessions. As the technical side was being managed by someone else they were free to concentrate on their fields of expertise, helping the students to decide upon content and structure and to experience the enthusiasm shown by most of the students.

During this phase, many students started to show their facility with visual thinking, and their knowledge of a broad range of techniques seen on MTV, in computer games, animated cartoons, and film and television in general. Editing techniques including filmic transitions such as fades, wipes and dissolves were attempted, not just for effect but to serve particular purposes. For example, one narrative used dissolves to erase characters in keeping with the plotline. Several productions (sports topics) introduced sequences of changing points of view to demonstrate action leading to outcome. One example, a mono-chrome production, included a very small, recurring object, a ribbon, in colour. In this instance the ribbon's trail was planned as an important visual story. It worked on the computer but failed completely in the printed version (monochrome).

Rough and undisciplined as almost all the efforts were, movement of and within the illustrations became a far more powerful means for conveying elements of the narrative than the printed word. Elements of the visual narrative in some examples were able to be read as sub-plots by peers. In one instance this was so strong that the text was no longer suitable. The attempt at rewriting resulted in a word narrative that lost its storyline flow. Read in isolation it was a narrative with important paragraphs missing, but read the way it was intended, via the computer, it became a story with considerable exploration of ways of adding depth, and more opportunity for alternative interpretations of meaning.

The introduction of speak text, sound effects and recorded speech provided opportunities to add further strength to the narratives. For the most part these were poorly used and the students were by and large not particularly enthusiastic about their achievements. Most were attempts at dialogue for characters. There was no evidence that any real thought had gone into any of these. Too often they were just parts of the original story narrative read aloud and then given to a character on the same page. The teachers expressed no enthusiasm for most of these additions. Student comments suggested that these had been included to hear their own voice, to have the computer talk and to prove to peers that they could do it. In many productions most of the audio was quietly deleted during the final laboratory session. The students were dissatisfied with their efforts because they perceived the dialogue to be a too immature comic-book style, even though their target audience might have been receptive to such a style.

As the range of options offered broadened beyond picture and text, some students became less confident about their ability to use these techniques. These students (mainly girls) turned back to their original work and concentrated on improving the quality of their pictures and the prose. They generally worked at this unobtrusively while participating in some of the general clusters and discussions occurring around the room.

At the end of it all, each pair of students left with at least two discs full of story material, and a hard copy of whatever elements of their work could be printed. Not all pairs completed the exercise to a level of readiness for presentation to their target children. A further opportunity was offered to these participants to complete the exercise under direction and with considerable modification. For the most part the printed version was seen as a disappointment. That there was too much missing was the most common complaint. Some thought that the paper version would make others think that they had spent weeks wasting time. Nine students were sufficiently dissatisfied with their print copies that they destroyed them at the conclusion of the final lab debriefing. More generally, students were concerned that they would not have access to a machine that would present their work properly. While this problem was addressed for the presentations to the younger children, no extended presentation option was offered by the school despite requests from parents and teachers.

Because the project was to take so much class time (one quarter of each fortnight's English allocation) the teachers wanted the productions to be marked in the conventional way so that the time spent on the activity could be justified both to parents and to the school administrators. As there were no available guidelines for marking, negotiation with the school administrators won a tentative agreement that descriptive assessment could be used, but it was made clear that this could be changed to a requirement for a mark, should the circumstances change as the project was in train. This negotiation about assessment represents a necessary collaborative challenge as we move towards new understandings of the changing nature of literacy. Towards the conclusion of the laboratory sessions the teachers were expressing confidence in marking the work according to a conventional marking scheme for writing. A descriptive assessment was applied to the use of the technology and to attempts to use animation and other options available only through the computer software.

This case study indicates teachers need to have clear understandings of the capacities of the technologies the students are using, as well as clearly defined curriculum goals which the technologies can support. Both are important conditions for effective teaching and learning of the new literacy. The case study also suggests that students' writing may no longer represent adequately the main evidence of their knowledge and effort in relation to learning this literacy.

Our second case study reports on the practices and beliefs of six English teachers and some of their students in using ICT for learning English in the years 1997 to 1998. These teachers' experience of English teaching varies from five to twenty years, and none had experience of using computers in class in English teaching prior to 1994. In the context of Australian state-funded schooling, Gold Secondary College is a resource-rich, regional school, with over 1,500 students enrolled in the Victorian Certificate of Education (VCE), a two-year study programme for 16- to 17-year-old senior secondary students. The VCE has a highly prescriptive curriculum, with specific work require-ments with both internal and external assessment of different tasks. In English, students are required to attempt a variety of literacy tasks, including a writing folio, responses to print and non-print texts, and the development of an analytical response to a topical issue. In analysing three or four other written viewpoints on this issue, students are expected to demonstrate analytical skills in evaluating the strengths and credibility of particular arguments and perspectives of other writers. They are also expected to develop a position paper or argument of their own on this issue.

The study design for English at this level is clearly intended, among various goals, to develop students' critical skills in assessing the style and merit of particular arguments on issues, but retains a strong linguistic rather than multimodal or multiliteracy focus. While students may comment on the format or layout of other commentaries and the value of accompanying illustrations or cartoons, work is assessed mainly in terms of engagement with the method and content of the written arguments. Students may choose to analyse a cartoon as a text, but assessment is again based on the content and linguistic strengths of this analysis. Similarly, work produced for the writing folio must be 'printable', thus ruling out submission of hypertext pieces for assessment. In this sense, the teachers' choice of particular technological applications for enhancing learning in English has been strongly driven by these curriculum prescriptions. While one teacher has encouraged student development of hypertext production, most teachers have strongly tailored staff or student work with technologies to address the learning goals of a curriculum that has a strong analytical, cognitive–linguistic flavour.

Since 1995 the College has implemented a whole-school approach to the use of ICT for learning across all areas of the curriculum. This approach is not easily summarized here but includes the following features. The College established a Local Area Network linked to all classrooms, a multi-media centre and a management structure to support and enhance ICT. All teachers and learning areas were provided with a baseline of equipment and software including 50 software packages, 60 CD-Roms, and access to the Internet. The College established a comprehensive website with all learning areas having a homepage, and teachers and students constructed personal homepages. All teachers were supplied with laptop computers with access to network and large television screens in classrooms, and all classrooms have access to Internet, intranet, library search engines, e-mail, network storage space and software packages. Students were given home access to electronic files, software, CD-Roms, Internet, intranet and e-mail. In 1998 the College had 350 Pentium PCs, and between two and six computers in each classroom. The College library was equipped with electronic search engines, and Internet sites were cached to support student study of particular topics in all subjects. Timetabling practices were restructured to include professional development as a core part of each teacher's role, and longer lesson times were introduced to enable more effective use of the new technologies. Collaborative approaches to teaching and learning were pursued through the College's intranet hosting of various discussion groups using Alta Vista as well as on-line listserv discussion groups. These web-based password-protected groups extended classroom interactions and interactions across different classes. Teachers' professional development in all learning areas was promoted through the development of technology plans in each learning area, and an initial focus on skills through inservice programmes, then a focus on learning models. Throughout this process teachers were encouraged to develop expertise and initiate new practices in, and take ownership of, these technological resources in developing their teaching and learning.

The six English teachers in this case study all participated in this whole-school approach to using technology for teaching and learning, and over the last three years have had experience with their students in using a variety of electronic technologies in English. An important part of developing these practices was continual opportunities to share experiences and to refine practices based on classroom success. Technologies used included digital cameras, Powerpoint presentations, Internet-based word processing, on-line text discussion with Alta Vista forum and on-line listserv groups, e-mail within Australian and international schools, publishing of individual homepages and word-processed student writing incorporating Internet images. There is not space here to report on the broad diversity of practices and combinations of technologies used by the teachers and students for varied purposes and with contrasting outcomes. However, we would like to focus on three particular practices as indicative of some of the issues associated with this learning. These practices are Powerpoint presentations, on-line text discussion and word-processed student writing incorporating Internet images.

Powerpoint presentations by both students and staff at the College have been widely used across many subjects in VCE, not just English. The English teachers considered Powerpoint to be a simple multi-media application that encourages the students to study set texts analytically. In producing Powerpoint presentations students need to select, organize and justify points about a text. This small-group work was also seen as promoting teamwork, co-operative processes in planning, and sharing of ideas. Students were required to present some work orally, with the Powerpoint as a focal point. By preparing a total package for an audience, students were forced to consider audience needs and to decide how the technology might enhance communication of their ideas.

In a typical activity, students in groups of four would be asked to research and give five-minute presentations to their class on one of six allocated topics regarding a set text. Each group was given a different focus and so became part of a jigsaw activity where presentations were intended to stimulate and consolidate analytical thinking on the text as a whole. Students are expected to examine the characterization and historical and social contexts of such texts as *Bladerunner*. The combined presentations were intended to enable students to explore how the cultural beliefs of a society influence the themes and narrative shape of such texts. Powerpoint presentations typically included summary points compiled by earlier whole-class or small-group discussion, information about the text obtained from books or the Internet, as well as images scanned from books or saved from the Internet to illustrate points. Teachers also used Powerpoint to present key points to students. For example, one teacher presented an analysis of *Bladerunner* interspersed with edited scenes from the film. Each Powerpoint slide contained a picture to represent the main focus on the scene being discussed, with written discussion points introduced when appropriate. Both teachers and students considered that this focus on detail enhanced learning. The students thought that the combination of visual and aural presentation, linked to opportunities for discussion, were effective in deepening their understanding of the text.

The English teachers believed that the use of Powerpoint strongly motivated students and also extended the range of ideas covered compared with past methods. In using the software, students were keen to incorporate information from a wide range of sources and were creative in attempting to improve their presentations, such as finding images to represent a kind of character, not necessarily the actor in the film. The teachers believed the presentations catered for a wide ability range, with lower ability groups encouraged to produce something worthwhile by the production quality achievable with this software. Able students were innovative in the ways they sought to extend the communicative possibilities of designing a set number of slides. These students were also forced to summarize material and identify key points because of the space constraints of this program. While some class time was used by the teachers to introduce some basic techniques for the programme, most students were sufficiently competent to work effectively on their own. The teachers calculated that no more than 25 per cent of time was used mastering the software when Powerpoint was first introduced.

Most of the teachers considered that many of their students had considerably more expertise in using new technologies than themselves. In this sense, students were often able to focus on the particular assessment outcomes, and used whatever worked rather than focusing on a particular technology feature. Easy access to the new technologies enabled students to explore and consolidate a range of new communication strategies which they demonstrated to teachers. The teachers thought the programme altered the way students learnt because they were now drawing on a far greater diversity of information. Students now had to make more decisions about relevance, credibility of sources, and communicative effectiveness in a software package that offered far more options than butcher's paper or other past technologies. As many have noted, the vastness of technological information sources necessitates that students develop critical research skills if they are to cope effectively. Increasingly, the teachers' role in using this technology was to set parameters, monitor and facilitate work, and to be the 'guide on the side' rather than showing students all the answers. The teachers thought that students learnt more effectively because they saw themselves as in charge of the design of their presentations. As one teacher noted, 'in the past we might have designed the golf course on which we expected the students to play, but now they are the designers'.

The students were generally very positive in their attitudes towards using this programme. They thought that selecting points, participating in discussion about the sequence of these points, and watching one another's presentations all enhanced their understanding of the texts. Their comments generally confirm the literature on the beneficial effects of technology on literacy learning, such as increased motivation, more pride in achievements and enhanced understanding.

The English teachers also use e-mail-based discussion groups for on-line text analysis, with the aim of encouraging more considered textual responses. Discussions were mainly conducted through Alta Vista Forum, a software program accessed individually by students via the school's intranet. Other discussion groups have been conducted through more open-ended use of e-mail with a student moderator (Jordan, in press). Once set up, the Alta Vista Forum discussion group continued up to the final essay examination on texts, with all comments remaining on the site, and hence available for scrutiny. The teachers considered that such discussion enables a wider range of perspectives to be considered than just in one class. Also, because contributors have to attach their names to comments, the teachers believe that this resulted in more considered and extended response than in face-to-face discussion. One structure used with Alta Vista entailed students brainstorming discussion points verbally and then using these points as the basis for on-line participation, with students expected to contribute at least four entries to their forum. Students were able to access the discussion group outside class time, and from different sites including the library or home.

The teachers thought that because students' ideas were 'on show' they put much more thought into their comments and took pride in what they had written. Their increased knowledge of the parameters of other students' thinking also encouraged them to form high expectations of the quality of thought being valued. While daunted at first by the procedures, students with less knowledge about computers soon became comfortable with the process. The teachers believed that the enhancing effects of this approach over usual discussion included the following: students could develop points without interruption or time constraints; they could deal with topics that might be uncomfortable to talk about; and they had the opportunity to revisit a point after more reflection or one that might have been lost in the speed of talk, therefore maintaining ongoing discussion with considered responses. Students also saw the activity as beneficial, not only for developing understanding, but also as a resource for exam preparation. They found the grouping of topics helpful, and understood the need for more considered responses. As one student commented:

> You want your comments to look good to other people and not silly so you put thought into what you are going to write. Reading other people's ideas on the same discussion point can help you sort out your own thoughts, and think of further ideas.

The third technology application on which we wish to report is word-processed student writing incorporating Internet images. Student use is monitored to address ethical issues of appropriate material. The English teachers used this technology mainly to support students' development of a writing folio. Students were asked to search the Internet for images or articles relevant to a topic. For example, one group of students, after visiting an art gallery exhibition on body images, wrote descriptive pieces about the images and emergent themes. They then searched the Internet for related images which they saved and incorporated to enhance their writing. Another group accessed and read articles on current world issues, in this case, the cloning of Dolly the sheep. Students then sifted information to prepare a word-processed piece of writing for their folio including visual material. In developing the skills of word processing, Internet-searching, and saving and integrating images, students were shown how to split the screen so that they had two documents (Internet search and their own essay) together on the screen. The teachers considered that this presentation in general approximated more closely to 'real' writing in newspapers and magazines. Commercial writing must compete strongly for attention and routinely uses visual enhancement, formatting and design features to grab the reader's attention. This suggests that future English teaching will entail more integration of media understandings and expanded notions of what counts as text.

The teachers thought that having convenient access to two texts, and in many cases a variety of images, encouraged the students to think more deeply about their ideas and how to represent them effectively. The teachers noted that some boys preferred to save lots of images and do little writing. Some girls wrote very effectively but were reluctant to find images. The teachers agreed that they had less control of what aspects in the texts the students were focusing on, but believed that this could be monitored and affected by individual attention to students. Some teachers commented that current assessment in this subject is too narrowly restricted to the written text alone, and that such a view does not recognize the multiple communicative possibilities of these technological programs. They believed that these restrictions need to change to acknowledge the complex effects of the technologies' capacities on communication. One teacher claimed that, 'we need to develop accepted ways of assessing the communicative impact of the whole piece, such as Web page design rather than just the written part'.

The teachers also perceived that students were changing the ways they worked in integrating technological procedures with image selection and text production. One teacher commented that the learning was different, in that students proceeded in less linear ways. Having chosen their images many students then went back and changed their writing. The teacher noted that 'seeing the image in front of them while they wrote helped to define what they wanted to describe'. While there were some possible dangers of lack of engagement by some students, teachers also commented that there was generally more collaboration between students, and more shared responses to what was found on the Internet. The students' perceptions of word-processed writing incorporating Internet images were also favourable. They enjoyed discovering museum homepages and commercial fashion advertising. They said that this work encouraged them to consider topics from different viewpoints and in more depth. They enjoyed varying the ways of developing and presenting work. For example, when working on body images they said that using the Internet pictures helped them to think further about their ideas when relating the Internet images to the art exhibits.

IMPLICATIONS AND THE FUTURE

Many issues arise from these two case studies in relation to effective use of technologies in learning literacy in secondary English. These issues include the major definitional question of the changing nature of literacy, given the diversification of what now counts for teachers as evidence of being literate. Certainly the perceptions and experiences of the staff and students in our case studies confirm new accounts of the nature of literacy proposed at the start of this chapter. Other issues concern new challenges in devising appropriate methods of assessment of learning this literacy, and the question of which teaching and learning practices are most effective in making students literate for a technologically saturated world. While these two case studies cannot be used to generalize about these issues, both studies support current perspectives in research literature.

Both studies confirm the view that being literate now must entail multiple communicative capacities including the ability to interpret and produce multimodal texts. Such a view necessarily implies that what counts as a text and its constituent parts needs to be enlarged or modified compared to traditional notions of text and textual structures. While we now have detailed accounts of the nature, structure and potential learning effects of traditional print-based writing (Bereiter and Scardamalia, 1987; Langer and Applebee, 1987), such accounts are yet to be developed fully about multimodal texts. Also, these new forms of texts invite author or producers to create texts that offer readers and viewers far more diversity of meanings and interpretive pathways than print-based texts. As evident in recent reports on national and state initiatives in Australia (Graham and Martin, 1998), there is a growing recognition that transparent norms need to be developed of what will count as success at different year levels in learning this new literacy. The legitimacy of diverse communicative structures and diverse technological resources for learning literacy needs to be acknowledged in state and National Curriculum documents on the goals and success indicators of student literacy learning. This is not to argue that the traditional goals of literacy learning have been completely supplanted, but rather that a richer conception of the nature of literacy, and how it will be achieved, needs to inform classroom practices.

A parallel issue relates to the professional development of teachers and the ways they can be supported in using new practices. As indicated in our case studies, the effective use of these new technologies represents significant new demands on teachers' expertise in structuring effective teaching and learning. While there is still much mapping of desired outcomes and appropriate teaching methods to be undertaken, our case studies reiterate some important principles about how this professional development might be achieved. Clearly there is a strong need for cross-curricular support and in-service programmes on how to use the options available. At the same time, literacy learning needs to be driven by clearly articulated curriculum learning goals for the subject, rather than be shaped primarily by technological opportunities or capacities. This does not mean that the technological resources do not affect what counts as literacy, but rather that these resources should not determine solely what is taught in English, and how. The case studies also indicate that this teacher development can be achieved by systematic collaboration between teams of teachers and by partnerships between schools and teacher education faculties that focus on classroom-based research into best practices. While we still do not have extensive research-based findings on which technologies best support particular or broad learning goals in secondary English, the development of such knowledge is likely to be achieved through collaborative work of the kind outlined in this chapter, and elsewhere in this book.

A further issue relates to the question of a critical dimension to literacy learning through the new technologies (Burbules, 1997a, 1997b; Prain, 1998). As noted by Lankshear, Bigum *et al.* (1997), and others, and also evident in our case studies, this dimension tends to be downplayed in current practices. However, there are very compelling reasons why literacy learning should focus on the issue of an ethics of usage. In a networked world it is imperative that future global citizens understand the effects on themselves and on others of these technological resources, and develop responsible attitudes towards, and practices in, their use. As Burbules (1997a) suggests, we can start by making our students aware of the design features of such technologies as the World Wide Web and explore how these features affect the purposes and meanings of what is produced.

Our case studies also raise the question of which teaching strategies are most effective in using the new technologies. Both case studies present examples of teacher-guided learning, with strong parameters used to frame goals, procedures and desired products for the activities, an approach that could be characterized as 'guided participation', as outlined at the start of this chapter. We do not believe that students should provide the major lead in literacy learning methods, even if their technical skills and knowledge are often more advanced than those of their teachers. Teachers do not have to know in advance all the pathways learners will take, but they do have to understand clearly the goals of the journey and also have some sense of the communicative possibilities of the technologies used, as well as possible pitfalls and distractions. The professional knowledge necessary to develop student literacy within and through these technologies is still in its emergent phase; this means that teachers need to build on their current understandings of effective literacy learning rather than give students too much licence to 'play' with the options or pursue their own interests.

In a recent extensive review of the literature on the relationship between knowing, learning and reasoning in the curriculum, Hofer and Pintrich (1997) argued that while there are common elements across all school subjects, each subject also has its own distinctive knowledges and practices. All the foregoing discussion in this chapter suggests that the current changes to the nature of literacy learning represent fundamental shifts in what should count as knowing, learning and reasoning in English. Print copies of work, as our case studies suggest, are no longer an adequate record of all student effort, knowledge or learning about texts. Also, there is much evidence, confirmed in our case studies, that boys and girls respond differently to these new literacy tasks, and hence pose new challenges for effective teaching and learning. The new technologies also pose many challenges in terms of time and resource management, and access for all. However, engaging with these challenges is absolutely essential if literacy learning is to be relevant to our students' needs and to the post-school world. A crucial starting place in thinking our way into all these issues is to learn from the experiences of other teachers, and to build on the understandings and practices of the kind reported in the case studies in this chapter.

Chapter 5

To Cope, to Contribute, to Control

JANE O'DONOGHUE

Most people cope, some contribute, and a few are in control. This truism can be applied to almost every aspect of our lives, from major political decision-making to moving house. With the advent of ICT, in particular the World Wide Web, there is, at last, a prospect of the accepted notion, where the majority are passive consumers rather than active producers, being reversed. With the Web, it's possible for everyone to contribute. Ultimately, we can foresee a world where those with the will, the skills and the confidence, will be able to exercise control over a specific domain or a wider area on the Web. By extension, they will also be able to take a dominant role in their society, as long as they are encouraged to do so. This chapter explores the reasons why English teachers should be offering that encouragement, and demonstrates how we can do so through a range of manageable and practical activities.

When I open a dictionary – a big, heavy dictionary of the kind that takes two hands to carry – I feel a surge of childlike excitement. Look how many words there are, look at the different combinations, look at how much there is to find out, just look ... the possibilities seem endless as every densely printed page yields several unknown words, and connections worm their way through the pages, suggesting the life and history of language. Perhaps, as I'm someone who enjoys words and takes pleasure in finding out about them and using them, this reaction will not be surprising. The reason for noting it is that this sense of adventure and excitement when faced with familiar but undiscovered territory is similar to the feeling generated by switching on the computer and entering the World Wide Web, especially if you've been there and enjoyed it in the past. And while we can cope with, use and re-organize the words offered up by that enormous dictionary, with the Web we are in a position to actively explore it, build on it, contribute to it and take control of it.

Not all of us will feel like this about the Web yet, but it is the future equivalent of one of those vast dictionaries. For some, logging on will be – like opening that huge book – an entirely new experience; for others it will be familiar and comforting, and the potential combinations, journeys and discoveries will be an exciting prospect. The desire to have all our English students feel about the World Wide Web the same way their English teachers feel about big dictionaries is a good starting point for thoughts about how we can use the Web in the English curriculum.

Despite rumours to the contrary, which seem to circulate particularly viciously in some English departments, getting on the Web is easy. Given a power point, a computer with a modem and basic keyboard and mouse skills, any individual can access the Internet. It's a democratic phenomenon worthy of the late twentieth century and beyond, bestowing publishing capacity on anyone with a few tools. English teachers with reluctant writers to motivate can take full advantage of such unprecedented opportunities.

The Web is also democratic in that it gives the average person access to information which in past times would have been regarded as privileged. (In 1998, for example, we saw the publication of Judge Zobel's pronouncement on Louise Woodward, a British nanny working in the USA accused of murdering her young charge. IPS News organized an on-line poll so that Internet users could air their own views, and a real-time chat room was provided by EarthWeb to discuss the Judge's ruling. Similarly, Independent Counsel Starr's report on the Clinton/Lewinsky affair became public property when it too was published on the Internet.) However, for the moment at least, the democracy of the Internet remains something of a myth. Surveys show that approximately 24 per cent of the UK adult population have used the Internet at work or at home, while about 16 per cent have experienced the Web and one-third of UK homes have personal computers (KPMG/Denton Hall Consumer Survey and KPMG, Ziff Davies, Yahoo! InternetTrak Survey, March 1998).

What is going to happen to those who do not have access to globally available information? Such access may be denied for many reasons, including fear of democracy, and the desire to control, but the most immediate problem is the expense. The *Times Educational Supplement* recently explored this problem in relation to school and family life:

> The barrier, however, remains the one which still generates the gap between the haves and have-nots – cost. A decent desktop computer still costs about £1,000 and a laptop half as much again.
>
> The danger is the creation of a group of children who have a computer at home to use whenever they like and those who can use one only at school – if they can ever get on to one. And that could affect their chances in life – a point not lost in the glossy advertising now being unleashed on families. (Johnston, 1998)

In schools, the problem of equal opportunity of access – which is actually about parity of learning across schools – is related to budgeting priorities and staff expertise. Secondary schools own an estimated one computer per 8.7 students (according to a British Educational Suppliers Association survey, based on 618 secondary schools in Britain and discussed in *TES Online* as above), but of course these are not distributed evenly around all schools. English teachers are used to compensating for inequalities in the education system and between individual pupils in the same class, providing books and other reading and research materials when school resources are limited, and for children who have no home access to such materials. Those same teachers, recognizing the unsatisfactory nature of the situation, will nevertheless be equally able to compensate for deficiencies and imperfections in ICT-based English teaching.

The consequences of the inequalities in ICT education are not within the realm of this chapter, but do serve to remind us of the importance of raising the profile of ICT in English in order to help schools stake a claim for proper provision. English is a subject whose responsibility in preparing students for the demands which will inevitably be placed on them in the future cannot be denied. More importantly, it is also a subject that can show students how to make those demands.

In Britain, and all over the world, English teachers have always been in the business of preparing students for the future, no matter what the current limitations of financial resources and equipment. Indeed, there's also a strong case for preparing students against the future. But the future is constantly changing, and as we move into the twenty-first century, the worlds of work, education, leisure, finance and trade will change more and more rapidly under the influence of technological capacities and the people who generate those capacities, that is, the students we are teaching now:

> . . . we need to see the English curriculum *not only* in its traditional role of *preparing students for* that future, but to see the curriculum, and the people who experience it, as *making and shaping* that future through their competent and confident action. (Kress, 1995)

As well as emphasizing the use of ICT and raising the profile of literacy and numeracy still further, the new English Curriculum document (expected in 2000) will address the theme of citizenship in line with the National Curriculum. This echoes Gunther Kress's appeal for the recognition of English as a central force in creating citizens who actively embrace and initiate change (*ibid.*, p. 13). If English is to do this effectively, it must subject ICT education to its own values. The aim must be to create English students who can use, produce and analyse ICT texts as well poetry, novels and newspaper articles, who can cope, contribute to and help to control. By exploring the four traditional modes of discourse in English, I will illustrate how this can be achieved.

WRITING AND THE WEB

If we take the term 'the Web' to encompass the Internet and the communication channels it provides, such as e-mail and chat forums, then it is easy to see how it makes demands on the user's writing skills. In time, voice-activated word-processing programs may usurp the importance of being able to physically process the written word onto screen, but for the moment at least, contributing to the Web depends on being able to write.

English teachers know about teaching writing. Once students have mastered the motor skills involved, we can provide a vast range of examples and stimuli to help them become more aware of their audience and create more interesting, integrated and effective pieces of writing. The Web not only offers us a plethora of additional sources for those examples and stimuli, but also supplies a ready-made publishing forum, where any child's work can be posted and celebrated, and often enhanced and given extra kudos by the graphics and layout of the chosen website.

However, the Web also offers us different ways of writing. Designing a website is a technical, but manageable, process requiring the designer to visualize text and graphics as integrated parts of a whole, emphasizing the significance of layout and audience response. The Web also allows students to see texts as layered and complex, not static and controlled:

> For centuries, the written word has had a central authority in society. Indeed it could be strongly argued that our notions of rationality and valid argument are all bound up with modes of thought that are derived from writing as a medium . . . The development of hypermedia represents a return to richer, pre-print modalities of expression . . . The opportunities it offers to speculate, to debate and to learn in more concrete, multi-sensory terms may have a deep significance in terms of what we are able to think about. (Cotton and Oliver, 1992)

With the Web, we are moving away from traditional notions of 'the written word' to an understanding of the written word as part of a wider matrix of communication, where writing is not necessarily more authoritative than other forms of communication, and when it is (e.g. in those legal judgements published on the Internet), it is more easily accessed and challenged. Appropriate use of ICT can help us to put students at the forefront of producing texts. This is both motivating and will help to redress the imbalance caused by years in which texts, especially literary texts, have been regarded as privileged and the product of emotions. By helping children to see texts as technical products of others and themselves, the Web can help us move away from the idea that if you can't feel something, you haven't got anything to write about. Writing for the Web, a student is not obliged to have an interior need to write, nor even to have an audience to write for. The fact that anyone can publish anything means that the notion of audience is denied, the concept of text is decentralized and the process itself becomes the focus.

In addition, writing with the Web can easily be a shared process: the clumsy accoutrements of collaborative writing in the classroom – large pieces of paper and fat, black markers, or the tedious swapping of pieces of paper which involves each writer exposing herself to the next – are replaced by the vision of a network of computers, in a single classroom or spread out around the country or the world. On the other hand, the fact that using pen and paper has now become a choice may allow us to value it more thoughtfully, reflecting on traditional writing techniques, and when pen and paper might be more appropriate communication tools than e-mail, phone, fax or a video-link.

Although assessment of writing is in some ways made more complex by ICT factors, it can also become a more real and purposeful activity when students are more willing to re-examine their own work, with a teacher, from a different perspective. A student looking back at a piece of writing on the Web and constantly available to others (not tucked in the back of an exercise book or filed in a folder) is distanced from the production process by its form and independent existence. This student can more readily adopt the position of the reader or audience, and is able to judge strengths and weaknesses with more clarity. The marking process will depend on the same questions (Has Donna matched her writing to the audience? Has Donna used interesting and adventurous vocabulary?) and some new ones (Has Donna used ICT to make her writing more suited to this format? Has she thought about the impact of design and graphology on her writing?). The assessment of collaborative writing requires the teacher to monitor the individual student's level of input carefully, but this type of work also offers opportunities for a shared and more constructive system of assessment than is sometimes possible in traditional contexts, with students recording and evaluating their own and others' responses to a task.

READING AND THE WEB

In the same way that the Web can refocus our attitude to writing, it will also change the way we read. The physical process of reading is one area where technical innovation is having an impact. Hotspots in websites tempt us with different colours and the lure of something more interesting, so that we no longer have to persevere with a dry or irrelevant page. Searching through text on-screen, which uses skills closely related to scanning and skim reading, is made easier and more effective through the use of a mouse to scroll through pages, and by search facilities provided by software and browsers.

Furthermore, reading in front of a screen is not such an isolating experience as reading a book, which can create a barrier between reader and text, and others. Anyone who has seen two or more students clustered around a computer screen reading from a website or a CD-Rom will have recognized the inherent intimacy of the experience. It becomes comparable to the experience of 'reading' films and other screen-based narratives, such as cartoons, documentaries and soap operas, in that it is shared and public. Yet when a group of children is reading a Web page, their responses are not inhibited by notions of etiquette and other conditions imposed by image-based narratives. From the English teacher's point of view, the reading experiences offered by the Web, CD-Roms and other screen texts are valuable precisely for their similarities with traditional modes of reading as documented by Montgomery *et al.* (1992, p. 192):

The reader can choose the speed of consumption (unlike for a film), and is not required by the environment to pay attention to the text to the same degree, so that variable levels of attention are possible. It is possible to skip parts of the text, and parts of the text can be re-read at the reader's convenience.

A Web page can be paused, scrolled forward and back, ignored, discussed, laughed at, replied to and criticized. What better method is there for witnessing children's responses to text? Compared to this sort of animated and vocal reading, silent reading in the classroom is alienating for the student and difficult to assess for the teacher.

The theory of reading may need adjusting to take into account the presence of the Web as an everyday tool in the teaching and learning of English, but in practical terms its influence is a simple and effective contribution to the current good practice of encouraging students to become critically engaged with a range of texts. In the past, we may have taught reading to enable our children to take part in a society which demands literacy, to bestow on them the pleasure of the novel, to allow them to pass exams or to understand job application forms. We may certainly have had more laudable, wide-ranging objectives than these, but we probably didn't think of reading as the interactive process it becomes when it is done through the medium of the Web. Its readers need to be able to judge when they are reading an original and valid page, and when they are reading a second-hand website about a website; they need to know how to electronically bookmark useful references and favourite sites; and how to find their way backwards and forwards around websites with many pages. Above all they need to know how to respond to what they read:

> ...I as the reader can, even with contemporarily available technologies, immediately make my reading visible in my re-writing of the initial/initiating text. This also diminishes (or nearly negates) the power of the writer: it is now – or can be – a mutual activity, in which reading has (very nearly) become real writing. (Kress, 1995, p. 23)

For Kress, the new reading process is one in which the boundaries between author and audience are blurred. If the audience can, with a few taps on a keyboard, respond to, annotate or even alter what they are reading, then the audience is as powerful as the author. This appears to take Barthes' theory of 'writerly' texts – innovative, demanding, non-conformist texts which require the reader to become involved in the process of decoding and therefore to take up a position of power within the author-text-reader process – to a new and unforeseen dimension.

Finally, reading is also changing because of the medium itself, and the impact it is having on text. Expert readers of the Web can not only manoeuvre their way around complex sites, select then manipulate text for their own purposes and respond to material in decisive, challenging ways; they are also readers of symbol and iconography. Logging on and using a server requires an understanding of menu bars and other visual tools, reading websites, e-mail and other ICT texts increasingly depends on one's ability to decode graphics and non-text characters.

SPEAKING AND LISTENING AND THE WEB

It is not only the boundaries between reading and writing that are blurred by the influence of the Web. More than any other medium, the Web also blends the theory and practice of speaking and listening with that of text-based forms of communication. However, for the purposes of English teaching, it is important to distinguish writing and reading on the Web from the activities related to e-mail and chat forums, which are generically linked to non-text-based means of communication, that is, speaking and listening. Just as the advent of new media during this century has caused us to reformulate our ideas about what constitutes reading and writing, so we are now rethinking the label 'speaking and listening'.

Some purists may regard it as improper, but to me, participating in e-mailing is the modern equivalent of a face-to-face conversation. The processes involved in sending and receiving an e-mail have strong links with those in which we take part during everyday conversation: decoding tone of 'voice', transience, speed, spontaneity, immediacy and informality are all central. In addition, e-mailers develop their own techniques for making communication quicker, easier and more individualized. A range of 'smileys' or 'emoticons' (symbols created by subverting keyboard functions for more creative purposes) is probably the most obvious form of dialect used by e-mailers, but there are also the various acronyms and abbreviations created and used in different chat-rooms by regular visitors making their messages quicker and more personal. (For an interesting range of emoticons and other e-mail forms, see the Online Glossary provided by Nan McCarthy in her cyber-romance series, *Chat, Connect and Crash*, published by Pocket Books, 1998.) Seeing e-mails and chat-room transcriptions as a form of written exchange denies their essential similarity to the way we communicate by voice.

However, as David Crystal (1998) has pointed out, 'none of the traditional notions of conversation analysis work well' for analysing web exchanges. This opens up the possibility of students creating their own means of encoding and decoding speaking and listening over the Web, and analysing the exchanges they find there. Close supervision will be necessary to allow them to take part in chat-groups, but such opportunities should be found and exploited, and a comparison of such an experience with more traditional forms of 'conversation' would be an interesting assignment in itself. To engage students in such an 'intertextual' exercise would recognize the value of informal and transitory communication in our current and future worlds, where something doesn't have to be written, recorded and indexed to be important.

It is possible to view electronic communication in a less positive way, and to ask students to consider the implications of a society in which daily, face-to-face meetings are inessential. As we head into the next millennium the media is brimming with eager predictions of a society which is not dominated by computers, and in which, instead, we take their presence, function and influence for granted. In such a society, they claim, employment as we know it will be a thing of the past and meeting your life partner will depend on having the right chip implanted rather than the accuracy of Cupid's arrows. (These and other predictions were made in 'Whatever Next?' an edited extract from *Next: A Vision of Our Lives in the Future* by Ira Matathia and Marian Salzman, published by HarperCollins, which appeared in The *Guardian*, 9 January 1999.) How will our everyday interactions take place there? According to one Internet enthusiast, 'the computer offers the illusion of companionship without the demands of friendship' (Turkle, 1996, p. 30). Our future expert Web-users will, presumably, need training in how to carry out effective exchanges with their machines as well as with the people they meet on the Web, at least to preserve that illusion.

In fact, the image of the Web as a globally oriented, isolating place is false, and e-mail and other aspects of the world of the Web can actually bring members of a community together. (An experiment by Microsoft 'to explore the social implications of electronic communications' was reported in the *TES Online Computers in Education Supplement,* 20 November 1998. More details at http://msnstreet.msn.co.uk.) In this and other respects, the study of new speaking and listening forms arising out of Web technology must be at the heart of any study of English, which claims to prepare students to be active participants, and contributing citizens, in the society of which they are members.

Like English, the Web is about reading, writing, speaking and listening. We can use it to find information, which can then be downloaded and reformulated. We can use it to publish ourselves, literally through a personal Web page, or in a more traditional sense through contributing ideas, poems, questions, criticisms and comments. We can use it to communicate with other individuals, in groups or pairs. We can use it to write collaboratively. (As others have pointed out, including Turkle – see above – the nomenclature here is disturbing: 'user' has negative connotations around addiction and dependence. But it is also a term which suggests the practical, transactional aspects of the Web, and it's a good name for the group of people who are not involved in the 'guts' of the computer industry, but are exploiting the possibilities it offers at screen level.) However we use it – and it will probably be in a combination of these ways, as the processes are rarely distinct – it is clear that English teachers have an important role to play in ensuring that future users are accomplished, confident and challenging of this new literacy.

DOWNLOADING INTO ENGLISH

The best thing about the Web is that you can look up millions of things at just a few clicks of a few buttons.

(Rebecca, 11)

The best thing is that you can get the latest system updates, like video drivers. And the latest music.

(James, 16)

I like the Web because it gives me the basketball from America, and you can find out information about anything. But now, nothing in your computer is safe.

(Benn, 16)

The Web is very convenient, fun and it offers lots of information on all my fave subjects. It is also good for homework.

(Laurence, 12)

My favourite activity is surfing for fun, because you can come across some interesting things you wouldn't normally look for.

(Vikki, 16)

On the Web, you can find info on anything, anywhere. But the ads and the repetition of the same info on so many sites is annoying.

(James, 17)

I like free-roaming all the sites.

(Ross, 12)

I like the Web because you can explore lots of stuff.

(Aktar, 15)

Although the Web's capacity for providing information to download is arguably its least groundbreaking quality, and to some extent merely mirrors other, readily available and less hi-tech research mechanisms, students are clearly more motivated by the idea of using it as a research tool than we might expect. Some of these children's comments provide an insight into the reasons why. They value the enormous and inconceivable potential that is 'out there'. They love the idea of the unexpected links and the freedom of search offered by simple clicking, beyond topic-defined book indexes and limited encyclopaedic entries. Conversely, they also recognize the convenience of being able to home in on very specific topics and use expert guidance provided by special-interest sites.

The job to be done in the English classroom, then, relates to building on these expressed interests and to making conventional information retrieval tactics relevant to the World Wide Web. The following tasks are simple activities for helping students with their first forays onto the Web for such purposes, and are designed to be integrated into the current English curriculum, rather than being 'add-ons'.

Revving up the search engine

A straightforward and valuable way to introduce students to searching the Web is to demonstrate the vastness of the material that exists on-line. Ask students to select a series of words – preferably nouns, but not necessarily proper nouns. They enter the chosen term into the search box and record the number of 'matches' indicated. This simple activity can be carried out on a stand-alone computer in pairs if whole-class access is limited, with an element of competition added if pairs compare the results of their searches. It could also lead to discussion of language, comparing the relevance of matches gained using words from different word classes. Do verbs generate as many matches? What about adjectives? Why is it useless to use a preposition as the basis of a search? Explain!

Defining and refining

This is a useful follow-up to the initial activity and shows students how to make a search relevant and use the Web pragmatically. An important skill in searching the Web is the ability to refine searches which involves thematic comprehension as well as technical searching and browsing skills specific to various search engines. Before beginning their searches, students need to think of a sequence of related words or concepts, all related to their choice of topic, but in descending order of specificity. For example:

Theatre	or:	Sport
Plays		Ballgames
Shakespeare		Football
Shakespeare's Comedies		World Cup
Twelfth Night		Brazil
Malvolio		Pelé

Entering these terms in descending order of specificity, and using the '+' key (or whichever refining mechanisms the search engine offers) to refine searches, will demonstrate the Web's vast capacity as well as the problems associated with browsing too vaguely or too specifically. A useful discussion about the advantages and disadvantages of the Web compared with other, more traditional forms of reference can help to engage pupils in a critical way with a relatively new medium. They need to be asking themselves when it's best to use the Web, and when it's not the most useful tool for the job.

This learning can then be consolidated with a further task requiring students to map their journey through the Web to a particular site. Their ability to describe the use of the Web can be tested by asking them to produce a set of instructions for another student to find the same place and answer a series of questions about what they find there.

Reading the Web

Too often in the early years of Web-based research, students are finding a good site, downloading and printing off a few pages, and handing them in: 'Here's my project on Victorian writers, Miss. Look how many pages there are!' Just as we wouldn't accept photocopied pages from a book, we also need to ensure that information accessed via the Web is processed and personalized if this is to be regarded as a valid form of classroom research.

Once students are confident about performing a search and have accessed some information that they need, the next step is to provide a reason for using the information, in a way which will require active reading. The traditional skills of skimming and scanning can be practised here, with students reading on-line, or at least on-screen, if at all possible. Mouse manipulation, using the scroll bar and understanding the value – or not – of hotspots are all key aspects of Web-reading. In this respect, the process is far more technically demanding than traditional reading; students must not be allowed to feel that the motor skills they use in Web-reading are somehow equivalent to, and negate the need for, inward digestion and comprehension of the information they find.

Compiling a guide to useful websites for other pupils is an effective way to practise Web-reading. The first stage will involve some preparation by teacher and students. They need to collate lists of recommended websites of the type which appear regularly in daily and weekend newspapers, and particularly in special-interest magazines. Such lists usually come with short, 'blurb' style previews and are interesting for the way they so obviously talk to a Web-literate audience. After the initial collection has been made, the class should deconstruct the features on these lists, looking for evidence of jargon and other writing characteristics, as well as design features relating to layout and presentation. In groups of two or three, students will need to select a topic – the areas of the school curriculum might be a particularly valid starting point for relevant choices. Research, in the form of browsing, note-taking and book-marking should then follow, with students using the search skills gained from previous activities. They will need to note the content, the accessibility, the reading age, the organization and the design of each site, perhaps awarding marks in each category. Ideally, the website guides can be published on the school website or intranet in an appropriate style for others' use at school and at home, and perhaps updated by teachers in each faculty or department, rather like a university reading list.

PUBLISHING AND INTERACTIVITY

I like editing my site and meeting different people.

(Joe, 12)

My favourite activity is playing Quake. It's fun and there is loads of blood and guts and it is very realistic and addictive. The worst thing about the Web is playing Red Alert.

(Steven, 14)

My favourite thing is creating my own page, because then you've got your own thing on there.

(Kim, 12)

My best thing is to play games over the net.

(Guy, 11)

The best things about the Web are multi-play, and that you can talk to people all over the world and e-mail only takes seconds.

(Salk, 15)

It's fun and creative and can be anything you like.

(Ryan, 12)

One of the paradoxes about the Web is that while it is often referred to as a 'virtual' world, it offers very real challenges. It also exists as a very vivid phenomenon in the minds of users, whether it is visualized as a fizzling network of wires, a pulsing bundle of electronic waves or a huge underground system of channels. As we already know from current good practice, writing, reading, speaking and listening activities that take place in real contexts, with a real audience and feedback that matters, are far more motivating and engaging than simulated tasks in which the only audience is the teacher. The Web provides that edge of reality.

Another aspect of the Web highly valued by students is the possibility of owning a slice of it. Web-authoring and publication packages are now easily available at a reasonable price, allowing students to create pages with text, video, sound and other animated links. However, designing a website involves making a series of decisions about form, audience and purpose, just like any other text-making process. The following tasks require students to start thinking about those decisions in small and manageable ways.

Bringing virtual reality into being
First, we need to help students to understand what the Web is. Explanations about telecommunications and modems are hardly inspiring, and seem to me to miss the point about the essentially amorphous nature of the medium. The Web is not something tangible to be picked up like a newspaper, or handled like a book, or even switched on and watched like a television. Instead, it's untouchable and abstract, yet strangely immediate and responsive.

A fun and creative activity to get students thinking actively about the Web is to ask them to represent it pictorially, and then to supplement their diagrammatic visions with Web-poems. A conventional form can be used here: ask students to think of as many ways as possible to complete the sentence 'The Web is . . .' with the focus on imaginative metaphors and similes. The following ideas all came from a Year 8 class:

The Web is a skyscape criss-crossed with flightpaths.
The Web is like a creature with a small head and lots of legs.
The Web is the biggest brainstorm in the world.
The Web is a huge sponge, leaking in all directions.

The Web is a giant spreading many-fingered hands around the world.
The Web is a mass of roots growing into cyberspace.

The results of this activity can be posted on the school's website, or e-mailed to one of the many sites now publishing children's work, and responses and other ideas can be requested.

Publishing a personal Web anthology

To help students consider the Web as a place where they can exist, to make them think about the range of the Web audience, and to simultaneously give them a chance to produce a page with a specific design, this activity is one that can be carried out independently or in groups, depending on the availability of equipment and resources.

A basic Web page template will be needed, which students should be encouraged to adapt for their own purposes. Basic categories for personal information will be needed (name, age, brief autobiographical details), but the main focus for the page will be categories relating to favourite choices of various art forms, details of which may be downloaded for use as desired. For example:

- Nineties pop song which makes me dance.
- Twentieth-century poem which gives me shivers up my spine.
- Extract from a Shakespeare play which paints a picture in my head.
- Pre-twentieth-century painting which makes me envious.
- Childhood book which makes me cry.
- Magazine which helps me laugh.
- Television programme which I never want to miss.
- Website which I am most obsessed by.

Having formulated their categories in this style, students need to create their Web pages to include appropriately formatted text, quotations, pictures and sounds to bring their choices to life. Font and layout should suit the context of each choice, with reference to period and mood. The end product should be a highly personalized and revealing insight into each individual. What could be considered as part of the evaluation of the activity is whether, as the page has been designed and created for exactly that purpose and for an audience of strangers, it is really a personal or a public document?

Interactive role-play

One of the most traditional and motivating activities we can ask students to engage in as part of the study of a text is easily updated into an effective and manageable Web activity, enabling children to publish and evaluate the process. The notion of writing in-role as a character from a play, as the author of a book or as a contemporary of a poet being studied offers a useful way of exploring any text, especially for the purposes of character analyses or investigation of a writer's style.

The most valuable way to launch this activity on the Web is to pair up with another school studying the same or linked texts – a school from as far away as possible adds to the sense of excitement about the project. This is not a one-off lesson and ideally needs to be ongoing for several weeks to allow students to experiment with a range of roles and to develop a correspondence. Students can work in groups as one character, with individuals providing alternative messages and then discussing and creating an agreed collaborative effort. The quality of the exchange will depend largely on the relevant teachers working together to agree ground rules about length, style and the focus of each 'letter'.

The range of texts which can be used as the stimulus for this activity is endless. Teachers working with older students on novels of Jane Austen might choose to forge a correspondence between the author and several characters from different novels. What would Catherine Morland (*Northanger Abbey*) have to say, for example, to young Lydia Bennet (*Pride and Prejudice*)? And what advice would Anne from *Persuasion* offer to these two? For younger pupils, an imaginary exchange between two authors with similar interests might be valuable. Two horror writers arguing over the best way to make readers quake, or two science fiction authors arguing over the possibility of life on Saturn would very usefully focus students' attention on matters of style and author intention.

COMMUNICATION

I like the way you can communicate and find out things.

(Lucy, 12)

I like visiting chat rooms to make friends, and to get to know other people.

(Eva, 12)

The best thing about the Web is that it gives you a chance to check out gossip, create your own page and everything – but the best thing is the chat rooms.

(Jo, 11)

The best thing about the Web is that you can chat to people on the other side of the world. And the worst thing is the junk mail on e-mail.

(Stefanie, 16)

I like sending e-mail – you get interesting conversations. The whole Web is interesting – NOT like reading a book.

(Andrew, 14)

The best thing about the Web is the huge variety of things to do. It's colourful and generally easy to use. I like visiting chat rooms because they are lively and you can talk to a whole room of people at one time.

(Jennifer, 14)

My favourite thing is chatting in the pub chat room because you can talk to different people and there are no hosts. The Web is fresh and there's an infinite amount of things to find out.

(Will, 16)

I like chat rooms. Everyone pretends to be drop-dead gorgeous and I take the mick!

(Kirsty, 16)

I use the net to talk to my American pen-pal.

(Charlotte, 15)

The best thing is the fact that you are linked with thousands of people across the world.

(Matt, 13)

I like sending e-mail because you get replies.

(Lucy, 12)

The best thing about the Internet is the chat rooms because you can be a totally different person when you're talking through the computer to different people.

(Alison, 12)

As these students have indicated, perhaps the most exciting aspect of the Web is its potential to bring us into contact with a wide range of other people. These pupils' comments celebrate the idea of a 'Web community' which shares access, interests and the ability to meet in what is currently, but doubtless will not always be, a rather elite environment. The simplicity and efficacy of e-mail is attractive: 'You get replies!' It's easy to empathize with this child's sense of frustration and disappointment at taking the time and effort to draft and write a letter, buy a stamp, post it and then *not* receive a reply! Lots of the children here also relish the international flavour of the Web, which English teachers must be sure to exploit in recognition of the importance of the increasingly global nature of our lives. However, the potential for more local chat is also significant. The nomenclature here is worth dwelling on for a moment, as the idea of 'chat' implies conversation on a rather superficial level, inconsequential gossip and irreverent exchange of views. But chat rooms can be used for more meaningful exchanges too.

Making Links
It should be the prerogative of the English department to establish regular use of the Web for exchange and communication, and an excellent starting point

for secondary and high school students is a link with schools for younger pupils. Large projects could extend to a page on the school's website designed specifically to introduce 'the big school', but smaller, more discrete tasks are a sensible way to begin seeing the Web as an effective method of communication.

A fruitful first activity is to design an e-mail questionnaire to send to local schools, with a view to surveying primary-aged pupils' attitudes and expectations of moving schools. Children can become highly engaged if there is a clear purpose for the questions, so they need to know in advance that the replies they receive will lead on to other activities. The questionnaire should ideally be preceded by an introductory letter, composed by class representatives after discussion, and might include questions about possible previous visits to the school, the exact nature of worries and concerns, what the younger pupils think will be different, what they already know about, and so on. As it is likely that the teacher will have a good idea what responses will be received, questions need to be generated by the students themselves, with discussion about types of questions and avoiding bias and confusion.

The questionnaire can, if necessary, be very simple: a list of questions which younger pupils take turns to answer before sending back their set of replies and deleting them so that the next child can respond. Alternatively, the respondents may work in groups. If more advanced resources are available, the questionnaire can include multiple choice answers, tick boxes and design features aimed specifically at the audience. Naturally, the researchers will be involved in decision-making about the reading and writing levels of their audience, and the information discovered – relating to both skills and interests – can be used to produce a leaflet (after leaflet analysis and discussion of persuasive and informative language) introducing the school to potential younger students. This is the sort of work that teachers have been doing with their classes for years, but with the Web and e-mail on hand to research styles of questions, provoke discussion about audience preferences and facilitate direct contact, such a project is enriched and, ultimately, more challenging and satisfying.

Instant gratification: messages and chat

' Checking out gossip'; being 'a totally different person'; talking to 'thousands of people across the world'. This is the element of the Web that students find most exciting. It is also, possibly, the aspect which teachers will find most daunting. However, one advantage to setting up school Web and e-mail links is that they provide rich ground in which to sow the seeds of links between individual children, which offers a vast range of possibilities for making ICT work for English teachers. Working with students who are accustomed to speaking and listening as a regular part of their English lessons, it is easy to observe their engagement, self-discipline and confidence. We must expect, therefore, that while we are in the process of introducing technological chat rooms and their conventions, advantages and disadvantages, there will be some over-enthusiasm and misuse. Purposeful contexts and focused activities can help to overcome feelings of panic and lack of control as we struggle to go beyond these first stages.

One way to make sure that chat takes place in a secure environment is to develop whole school and class links in order to pair up individuals or pairs with others for a reason. For example, pairs in a class who have already taken part in the questionnaire and research activity can work together with pairs in the younger class, with topics (relevant to class work) provided for chat in a given time slot. Alternatively, to focus on form rather than content, the teacher may wish to allow a more free-ranging discussion which can then be printed off and discussed as an example of 'talk'. Chat rooms set up by the teacher can include any number of participants, and the role of 'host' can be given to another pupil.

Another possibility is to organize on-line meetings with the various authors, actors and other celebrity figures who now have their own websites or take part in Web events to which schools can sign up. To make the most of such opportunities, students need to be well prepared and a follow-up task will help give the activity a context and purpose. For example, over the course of a school year, groups of children in a class can take turns to talk to a number of authors. The final product might be an addition to the school's website in the form of an introduction to each author, a bibliography, a summary of questions asked and answers received, and some book recommendations relating to each.

As I suggested earlier, the role of chat using ICT is essential to the way English teachers develop children's speaking and listening skills for the future. The responses of the students I questioned about their uses of the Web, in all its forms, focused very strongly on its provision of powerful, new, effective ways of communicating with others. Given that speaking and listening skills are, for most of us, our most used and most important methods of communication, I was heartened by the way in which those students embraced and celebrated their membership of the chat world. Perhaps it's because they don't view chat in the same way as they view classroom talk; hopefully, in the future, they will. Hopefully too, they'll be very good at it.

CONCLUSION: TOWARDS CONTROL

One helpful way of understanding how the three areas of the Web can enrich the English curriculum is to examine the possibilities and limitations of each. Reading the Web for information, searching and downloading is the first, most familiar stage. Like knowing the alphabet in order to look something up in that huge dictionary, the basic skills students require for this activity will allow them to cope with its vast offerings and consume some of its menu. One step on, and with the additional skills which enable them to contribute, students will be able to interact with this new forum, to participate in the pleasures and challenges it offers.

The final stages of students learning about the Web are about knowing how to handle the form as well as the information, and being able to participate through critical communication. If English teachers can provide the means and the inspiration to enable students to take control, to become enthusiastic, expert and innovative producers, not passive consumers, then we will have gone some way towards providing an English education for the next century.

Chapter 6

Computer Games as Literature

DON ZANCANELLA, LESLIE HALL AND PENNY PENCE

> It was so immersive to me, so powerful because I became a part of a different world, a world where my participation, my courage, my dedication were vital, crucial to the world's continued existence. A world where I was being evaluated mostly on how hard I was willing to try and how clever I could be. And that was pretty much it.
>
> (20-year-old describing his early experiences with a video game)

Among the most important shifts in thinking about the subject of English during the past ten or fifteen years has been the gradual move away from placing literature at the core of the curriculum – as the study of privileged texts as static objects – and the accompanying move toward the study of many different kinds of narrative and linguistic experience, from popular fiction to advertising to film. As Robert Scholes argues in his book *Textual Power* (1985), 'What students need from us ... is the kind of knowledge and skill that will enable them to make sense of their worlds, to determine their own interests, both individual and collective, to see through the manipulations of all sorts of texts in all sorts of media, and to express their own views in some appropriate manner' (pp. 15–16). Or, to put it more directly, 'we must stop "teaching literature" and start "studying texts"' (p. 16). However, for all the sympathy the teaching community has had for this shift (and even the more traditional and conservative of us seem willing to consider the validity of, for example, the study of film), the majority of teachers would probably stop short of viewing computer or video games as texts worthy of much serious attention in the classroom.

In fact, it's difficult to think of a category or type of text that has less cultural status and invites more adult disapproval than console games.[1] Parents frown when children spend hours in front of the screen, fingers flicking in what to adult eyes seem to be random movements as images flash brightly across the screen. The parents of the young man with whom we introduced this chapter periodically prohibited him from playing because he became so immersed in his game that he was late for school or didn't complete his household duties. As teachers, we have an easier strategy for dealing with these outlaw texts: we simply act as if such texts don't exist. We teach paper-print literature[2] and perhaps a little film, all the while bemoaning the fact that our students don't read as much as we did, wondering why they don't race home to their novels, when in fact they race home to texts that are meaningful to them – their console games. If we use Scholes as our guide, however, we are pointed toward a more serious consideration of such texts – because to do so might 'enable [our students] to make sense of their worlds' and become better readers of a kind of text that may well play as large or larger a role in their lives than books and newspapers and magazines.

Buckingham and Sefton-Green (1994) in *Cultural Studies Goes to School* point out that 'the popularity of computer games has brought about a fundamental change in notions of reading and authorship' (p. 215). We believe that one way to investigate these changing notions of reading and authorship is to respond to and reflect on these games as works of literature, to approach the playing of these games as a literary experience. Louise Rosenblatt in her book *The Reader, The Text, The Poem* (1978) characterizes the literary or aesthetic experience as a 'lived through' event:

> Sensing, feeling, imagining, thinking under the stimulus of the words, the reader who adopts the aesthetic attitude feels no compulsion other than to apprehend what goes on during this process, to concentrate on the complex structure of experience that he is shaping and that becomes for him the poem, the story, the play symbolized by the text. (p. 26)

She argues that it is important for the reader to attend 'to the actual experiences that the text signals' before attending to 'the analytic classification of the types of character or intricacies of plot that might be outlined'. This immersion in the world of the text is an essential prerequisite for discussions of feelings, characters, events, tensions of dialogue and action, form, and meaning. When conducting these discussions, it is important to consider the background and skills each person brings to a given text and the socio-cultural context surrounding and contributing to a reader's response. The application of Rosenblatt's notion for media studies is similar to its implications for the study of paper-print text – that allowing students first to experience, and then to reflect on their personal experience, is an essential first step for meaningful analytical study of texts.

In the spirit of Scholes and Rosenblatt, then, the three of us, two teachers of English and one teacher of technology with a background in elementary school teaching, have been trying to 'adopt an aesthetic attitude' toward console games. We have attempted to approach them not as games to be won or puzzles to be solved, but rather as complex texts that can evoke lived-through experiences. We have attempted to recategorize (Bazalgette, 1992) these games as literature, that is, as texts that allow us, as print literature has historically done, to enter into created worlds, to participate in and reflect on realities other than our own, using the personal meaning we create through 'reading' these texts as a stepping-off point for more critical analysis.

READING THE TEXTS (PLAYING THE GAMES)

To illustrate our literature-based approach, we will focus on three games, all of which can be generally categorized as role-playing, adventure or conceptual simulation games.[3] That is, the players (we'll drop here the 'reader/player' locution, our point being that playing and reading are one and the same), assume the identity of, or accompany a character into and through, the world created by the game. Because of our interest in approaching these games as literature, we have purposely chosen games that exhibit aspects of narratives. The primary goals of the games we have selected are to engage players in understanding particular situations, developing characters, and problem-solving, rather than to engage in combat. We have not included 'beat-em up', shooting gallery, or platform games, although we will later argue that a literary stance toward these combat-oriented games might also be useful.

All three games are CD-Rom programs for either IBM or Apple Macintosh computers. Games of these types are played fairly widely by many young people. All three are for sale on the commercial (as opposed to educational) software market, although *Oregon Trail* is also popular in American schools because of its focus on the period of westward expansion in nineteenth-century American history. We present them as vehicles for demonstrating a literary approach rather than as evaluations of particular software.

To represent our literary way of reading, we will describe our experiences with each of these games, sharing with you our responses based on our own backgrounds, perspectives, personalities and expertise. Hence, we shift to 'I' voices below, as Penny describes her experiences with *Riven*, Don, his experiences with *Rockett's New School*, and Leslie, her experiences with *Oregon Trail*. After we have dealt with each of these games individually, we will shift back to our unified voice to share with you what we have learned about console games as literature and to ponder some implications of what we have learned for English and media literacy instruction. And so – let the games begin.

PENNY PLAYS RIVEN

I do not usually play console games. I tried numerous times to get involved with my children's enthusiasm for the Mario Brothers and combat-oriented games in the early days of Nintendo, but I found none of those games intriguing or relaxing to play. I enjoyed watching the screen as my children played but felt too stressed-out when I played to consider it fun. I would find my shoulders hunched and my fingers cramped after just a few moments of play. However, when I came across the December 1998, *Macworld*'s hall of fame list, I found a review of a pair of games that piqued my interest. The reviewer characterized the games as follows:

> Less like computer games than like wonderfully illustrated novels, both *Myst* and *Riven* transport you to a world where deciphering where you are – and why you're there – is all part of the fun. While both games lead you toward a final goal, the true point of *Myst* and *Riven* is to explore the gorgeously rendered worlds and the characters that live in them. (Crotty 1998, p. 73)

They also recommended them to people who 'enjoy beautiful graphics, brain-teasing puzzles and games that don't induce too much stress' (p. 73). As a lover of novels, I was intrigued. I bought the worlds of *Myst* and *Riven*.[4] After a fairly simple loading process, I entered the world of *Riven*. What I found there was a richer literary experience than I had anticipated. In the following section I relate some of this experience in the present tense in order to try to convey to you the immediacy that I felt as I played.

My reading experience
I begin my journey, using only the basic directions in the User's Manual (Cyan, 1998). After a short, introductory sequence of beautiful graphics, I find myself sitting face to face with a man whom I don't know, but who seems to know me. He looks up from his writing and says, 'Thank God you've returned. I need your help.' He hands me a book and explains that all I need to know is in there, that I need to keep it hidden. He then hands me another book, a Linking Book, which he calls a one-man prison. He explains that I will need it to capture Gehn. He also instructs me to find Catherine and signal him when I do. At that point, he will come with another Linking Book and bring us back, and, if all goes well, he can get me back to the place where I came from.

At this point, I understand that I am to enter the world of *Riven* with a task to complete – capture Gehn and find Catherine. I also understand, because of the weightiness of his tone and the darkness of our surroundings, that the adventure on which I am embarking is serious business. But I have so many questions – Why am I here? Who is Gehn? Why does he need capturing? Who is Catherine? Why does she need finding? How and why did she get lost? What is a Linking Book? What is the other book? What will happen next?

As if in answer to my silent questions, I find myself in a lighter space, looking out among steep rock walls; a tall metal object, reminiscent in shape of an inverted ice-cream cone is to my left, among the walls, but before I have a chance to even think about moving, bars arise in front of me, grinding to a close, locking me in. A few seconds later, a man dressed in a worn white coat, tan trousers and knee-high leather moccasins appears in front of my cage. His hair is long and dark, and he wears a white helmet. He startles when he turns and sees me in the cage. He speaks to me in a language I can't understand. He becomes frustrated, reaches into the cage and steals one of the books; I am not sure which one. He opens and peers into the book. But when he leans forward to read, he grabs his neck in pain and falls to the ground, unconscious. He is dragged off by an unseen force or person. In another few moments, a second man appears, dressed in a camouflage jacket with a red sash and goggles. He picks up the book. I'm not sure, but I think he smashes it as he kneels to move a lever that opens the bars to my cage. He runs off. A small hand appears in the centre of the screen, and I am free to move about. The hand is attached to my mouse and, by moving the hand and clicking, I can move out onto the landscape. I can also push buttons, pull levers, and examine and use objects in my exploration of this world, a world of rich well-worn textures, soft colours, and vibrant noises.

At this point, I am following the User's Manual directions, which offer basic movement and manipulation techniques, which I find suggestive rather than clarifying. For example, the directions for playing the game begin with the following passage:

> An old D'ni proverb reads, 'Lose your questions and you will find your answers'. *Riven* is a continuation of the story from the *Myst* CD-Rom and the *Myst* novels. The secret to *Riven* is that are no secrets! Become lost in the beauty of its worlds and think as if you were actually there. Take time to explore and pay close attention to the details in the worlds; don't overlook anything. Keeping brief notes may help remind you of important clues and information you encounter along the way. Think about what you have seen in other parts of *Riven* and logically piece together everything you know.

At this point, I am struck by how little I know about the logic of such an environment, by how little background I have because I am not familiar with *Myst*. My movements are random. I have been advised to keep a journal of my experience (and a very nice one is provided), but I can't even understand what I am supposed to be doing – or even if I want to be doing it. In spite of my increasing frustration, I find myself interested in this new, visually enticing environment. I am not just watching over someone's shoulder or peering through someone else's eyes; I am a character in this story. I see other people; they talk to me. I can't talk back, but I decide in what direction I will move, what I will pick up, what I will open, what I will close, what I will examine closely. I can move forward through this visual text, and revisit parts I have already experienced. I am able to get lost in the exploration.

I move among the steep rock walls, look out over expansive vistas, walk across rope and wood bridges. I enter dark tunnels and walk towards the light, exploring rooms within the rock. One room contains a throne-like seat with a cage around it. I can open the cage and sit on the seat. Another room contains a series of columns, and on each column is a beetle. I open a beetle's wings and peer into its centre and find a golden stained-glass window with a book in the centre and people bowing down. Tree stumps surround it. I open another and find a similar window, a man with a halo sitting at a desk and writing. I open other windows – a man with a book on his head, like a halo, with people kneeling before him in supplication; a man falling into a fissure in the earth, with the book in flames; a man giving paper and a book to the people. This room is very beautiful to me, and the windows call up images of church, but I don't know what the pictures mean, nor do I know what to do in the room. I move to another room and find strange, insect-like statues with gem-like eyes and a pile of gems beneath them, positioned on either side of an elliptical cage. It is fairly quiet and peaceful, but I feel a sense of urgency, a sense of mystery, and I don't know what to do.

Because I want to know more, I turn to a second print text – the *Official Player's Guide*. The six chapters of the *Player's Guide* (Keith and Barton, 1997) offer increasingly more specific directions for solving the puzzle of *Riven* and are marked with creatures that can be found there to symbolize the amount of information about the game revealed. Chapters 1 and 2 offer some general advice on 'Roaming Through Riven' (p. 7); Chapters 3, 4 and 5 help you navigate the islands and solve the puzzles and problems that lead to successfully completing your mission of capturing Gehn and finding Catherine. Chapter 6 walks you through one path toward completing the game.

In Chapter 3, I find out that the place where I started my quest was called Temple Island. It recapitulates the opening scene. I find out that the second man took the Trap Book, and what he smashed was not the book, but the lever to my cage. I am also asked to consider a list of questions about this scene:

- Does all of this tell you anything about the people of Riven?
- The first man wears a uniform, though it looks more like it is wearing him.
- Does that tell you anything about a local government or power structure?
- He's attacked by someone who moves cautiously, a guerrilla or rebel. What does that tell you about Rivenese society? (p. 14)

Okay, so the man who spoke to me was a soldier of some sort, and the man who opened the cage was a rebel. Riven must be in some kind of civil war. I must be on the rebel's side, since he was the one who saved me. They must be rebelling against Gehn, because I am there to capture him, but why are they rebelling, why do they need my help, and how can I find Gehn through this maze of rooms and gadgets?

As I continue to explore with the limited information in Chapter 3, I notice an icon for a book, which turns out to be the journal that Atrus (I have figured out that he was the man in the opening scene) gave me. The journal, dated 78.6.10 and written on parchment in fountain pen or quill, seems timeless. By reading it I find out some of the history of this struggle:

They held for more than thirty years, but the corrections I made to Riven have finally failed – the island has resumed the familiar pattern of decay that is the hallmark of my father's work. I must now race to implement this new patch before it's too late.

Aha, Gehn must be Atrus' father, and Riven is a world that is constructed or at least manipulated in a tug of war between Atrus and Gehn. I find out that Gehn is driven by his 'myopic mission to restore the D'ni civilization' and that his efforts have 'left too many innocent cultures dying in its wake, and would continue to do so, were he to once again be free of the confines of Riven'. Atrus feels responsible for all the people of Riven and seeks to evacuate them and keep Gehn trapped.

I further discover the role of books, and the stained glass starts to make more sense. Books allow people to be transported to different worlds. When someone else uses a book, the first person is displaced. If the connection is partially severed, the person who uses it will be 'permanently trapped in the dark void of the Link'. I now realize that I have been transported via a Linking Book and better understand what Atrus meant when he said, 'If all goes well' in the opening scene. I am just beginning my journey, and I still have many questions, the largest still related to the reasons I am here, but I have surrendered to the tale and am committed to constructing myself in this new world.

Reflections on meaning
In *The Making of Riven* (Cyan, 1998), the movie that accompanied my version, Rand and Robyn Miller, the developers, explain what they were trying to do. They wanted to build 'a place we'd want to go to', a place that 'makes you take a step back from the world and makes you think about the place you're in'. I found that the game allowed me to stop and think, not only about the virtual world that they created, but also about the world we, as a society, have created.

To make meaning of the situation in which I found myself in this game, I moved among different kinds of texts. In animated texts, I moved from one place to another and manipulated objects within that scene; I watched other characters in movie-like intervals, and I was a participant in conversations with other characters, albeit my participation was limited to my thoughts as someone talks to me. It was interesting; rather than take on the role of someone else, it was more like I was myself in this new world. I was not encouraged to take on a role other than to be who I am. I was required to act on things that I encountered and to make decisions in order to complete my quest, but I felt like it was I who was in this world; I didn't have to identify with a character, I *was* the character.

As I moved through and reflected on the world in which I had entered, I found that the Linking Books were symbolic, that they represented the ancient D'ni culture's ability to enter into other worlds through books. Gehn, in his unrelenting desire to reconstruct that culture, was in some way dominating Riven, using its precious resources to make books – hence the stained-glass windows depicting the giving of books to the Rivenese, their worship of the book surrounded by tree stumps, and the importance of the Linking Book that I was given to enter Riven. The game seems not only to be about puzzle-solving but also evokes a commentary on cultural preservation and its cost. I am still immersed in the world of *Riven*. Surprisingly, I am fascinated by this new world. I have, of course, ordered my copy of *Myst*, the precursor to *Riven* and am reading *Myst* (Miller and Miller, 1995), the print novel that serves as a prequel to the computer game. Through these other related texts, I am learning more about what it means to observe and make meaning in this world. I am in no hurry; I am enjoying finding out more and more about this world through whatever means necessary. This computer game, for me, has become more of an invitation for further exploration, rather than a challenge to get to the end. After all, I know that there are several possible endings and that I can play the game again to arrive at a different one. In *Riven*, I am experiencing a work of literature in which the journey has become more important than the outcome.

DON PLAYS *ROCKETT'S NEW SCHOOL*

The cover of *Rockett's New School* describes this CD game as a 'Friendship Adventure for Girls, Ages 8–12'. Amidst cartoon-character faces of pre-teen girls float the phrases 'Meet cool friends', 'Peek into lockers', 'Make choices that change what happens', and 'It's your first day ... What will you make of it?'.

As the game begins, I find myself in the company of a girl named Rockett who is a new student just beginning her first day of school at Whispering Pines Middle School. As with most role-playing computer games, the player follows the lead character through the world offered by the game – in this case, a middle- to upper-middle-class-looking school – determining with a click of the mouse what choices the character will make. The focus on the game is, as one would expect given the 'New School' theme, making friends. At various points in Rockett's day, she is faced with decisions about how to respond to the people she meets, the implicit goal being the building of relationships with other students. For example, shortly after she arrives at school, Rockett is sitting on a bench just outside the front doors of the building when another girl joins her. They strike up a conversation and then the girl asks if Rockett wants to accompany her inside. Rockett has to decide – is this a person she wants to cast her lot with so early in the day (the girl seems a bit self-centred) or should she politely decline? At that point the screen changes from a view of Rockett and the girl in front of the school to a view of three different 'Rocketts' – one with a frown on her face, one with a smile, and one looking thoughtful. As I touch a face with the cursor, Rockett's voice offers choices – the frowning Rockett explains that she doesn't like the girl and feels imposed upon; the smiling Rockett explains that the girl seems nice and that she wants to be her friend; the thoughtful Rockett decides to ask to meet up with the girl later but to go it alone for now. I click my mouse on the thoughtful Rockett and the story continues, along a different path than if I'd have made either of the other choices.

Later, during lunch, Rockett must decide where to sit. She has already begun to understand the social order of the school and has to make a decision about her place in it. Should she try to be part of the popular crowd, despite her sense that they are shallow and exclusionary? Should she befriend a girl no one seems to like? Or should she approach a boy who seems interested in talking to her. Again, the three Rocketts appear and I make my choice.

For the most part, *Rockett's New School* is very traditional in its use of character and narrative structure. The plot is episodic – the highs and lows of Rockett's day – and linear/chronological: we follow Rockett from the moment she walks in the doors of the school, through her first class period, the passing periods between classes, on into lunch, and so on. We are always with the heroine, accompanying her in almost the same way we accompany characters in books written with limited omniscient narration. There are, in fact, extended passages of pure narrative during which the experience of the disc is very similar to the experience of watching a movie, albeit an animated movie with rather limited animation. My tendency as a reader during those sections was to sit back and watch, feeling myself almost slip into a TV watcher's state of mind. I say almost because the narrative is continually interrupted by the moments when the three Rocketts appear on the screen and I have to choose what do to next. There is a certain predictability to choices – one choice is usually very timid, a second very self-assured, and a third almost mean-spirited or resistant.

Beyond the central narrative and repeated opportunities to choose the path the narrative takes, there are hypertextual elements in Rockett's world which are accessed by clicking on the icon of her book pack. The frame is then filled with her bulging pack, from which protrude her diary, her sketch book, and a 'Look into lockers' padlock which, when clicked, causes a bank of lockers to appear, each of which has on it the name of one of the characters Rockett meets during the course of the day. Click on a locker and one learns about the 'inner' life of her new classmates – from Cleve's strained relationship with his absent father to the amount of time and effort Nicole devotes to her appearance. The majority of information available through the book pack is written – journals, letters, school papers, notes from teachers, etc. – so that this aspect of *Rockett's New School* is highly print-oriented – so much so that moving from the primary cartoon narrative to the book pack is almost like moving from television to a parallel epistolary novel. Characters become much more nuanced and multidimensional. We even have access to teacher mailboxes where we learn about their perceptions of students, as well as catching glimpses of the adults' lives away from school – a feature often played for laughs but also sometimes poignant and revealing.

On the whole, the experience of playing *Rockett* is much like participating in an interactive TV drama aimed at pre-teens. The interactions are limited and circumscribed, but the situations are authentic and engaging. This is a game which has clear roots in conventional dramatic and fictional forms, but which also suggests some of the possibilities that moving such narratives to the computer can provide.

LESLIE PLAYS *OREGON TRAIL*

In its various versions, *Oregon Trail II* (MECC, 1997), one of the most popular pieces of educational software in American schools, has occupied school children for over twenty years. This simulation, recommended for grades 5–12, lets students 'experience U.S. history firsthand as they travel the Oregon, California, and Mormon Trails as an emigrant, facing daily danger while bringing a wagon party across the continent' (p. 2).

During my years as an elementary school teacher, I taught American history. My students were generally the children of Hispanic migrant farm workers. The history in our social studies textbooks was not the history of my students. I continually pointed this out to them and brought in alternative materials and viewpoints to help them understand the subjectivity of history. This is not the way most children experience history in schools.

The school version of *Oregon Trail II* is similar to the kinds of materials students encounter in social studies textbooks. The simulation offers classroom teachers many support materials to help prepare students for the decisions they will be required to make along the Trail. A companion piece of software, *Writing Along the Oregon Trail* (MECC, 1994), recommended for grades 4–8, provides opportunities to engage with issues such as Manifest Destiny, the slaughtering of bison herds, and the effects of mass migration on the environment. The simulation covers the time period of 1840 to 1860, which saw rapid expansion into the American West. The objective of the simulation is to reach Oregon Territory safely with the family in good health in order to increase options for economic success. While making preparations for beginning the journey, I had to decide on an occupation. The professions available to me were those held by men during the time period. I could not choose my gender or race as the leader of my party was male and white. I also had to choose or name the other four members of my party, decide on one of four cities as my jumping-off point, and purchase supplies.

On the Trail, I experienced the common hazards of transcontinental travel during the time: accidents, illness, injuries, river crossings, lame animals, broken wagon parts and adverse weather conditions. The decisions I was required to make were those which would have been made by male members of a party. The simulation did not offer me opportunities to experience the Trail as women would have experienced it or to confront the challenges women of the time would have confronted. Although some activities included examining the diversity of people along the trails, researching Native American tribes that might be encountered, and role-playing the part of a Native American, I found the treatment of these topics to be somewhat superficial. As a player of *Oregon Trail II*, I was sometimes positioned as an active participant in events; at other times I was simply an observer. The graphics displayed signalled to me what my positionality was to be in any given context. When I purchased my supplies and listened to characters who gave me advice about potential hazards, the screen offered me the point of view of my character. When travelling the trail, I became an omniscient viewer of my wagon travelling through various landscapes representative of the actual terrain of the American West.

Semiotic theories of response used to analyse *Oregon Trail II* bring up the issues of readers' responses to stories told through different media and to intertextuality. Beach (1993) states that in order to understand diversity in our responses to various media, it is important to explore the same content as portrayed in several media. This will help us realize how the unique characteristics of a medium can influence our response to content. Clearly, the producers of the software package *Oregon Trail II* intended for me to experience the story of the American Westward Movement in a different way than I would through a social studies textbook, personal diaries of the trip, or even a fictional, paper-based account of the journey.

Actual classroom use
In his introduction to *Past Imperfect: History According to the Movies,* Mark C. Carnes (1996) notes, 'Hollywood History sparkles because it is so morally unambiguous, so devoid of tedious complexity, so *perfect*' (p. 9, emphasis in original). The same could be said about history according to *Oregon Trail II.* The simulation offers classroom teachers many support materials to help prepare students for the decisions they will be required to make along the Trail. The publishers note that over 200 primary and secondary sources were consulted during the researching for this simulation, thus ensuring historical and geographical accuracy. Over fifty of these sources are listed in the Bibliography section of the accompanying materials. But even if teachers utilize the support materials supplied by the publisher, students experience a very sanitized version of the American Westward Movement. Genocide, women's roles, destruction of the environment, and race relations are glossed over.

In reality, very few American teachers use the simulation in the ways that would help students make sense of the content through this new form of text. In most classrooms, the software is loaded onto the classroom computer and students play the game in their spare time. One favourite activity of students is to purchase as much ammunition as possible so they can shoot game at every opportunity. Since the amount of food that can be carried in the wagon is limited, much of the slain game is left behind. Of course, this is what happened during the first half of the nineteenth century. Buffalo hunters, explorers and settlers wantonly decimated the bison herds of the West. Many Native Americans starved as a result. It is troubling to me that the game never affords students the opportunity to see the consequences of their slaughter within the game environment, allowing them to be as blind as the early emigrants about the impact of their presence, attitudes and actions on Native Americans and the environment.

Analysis

Wolf (1988) argues that readers generally experience texts as unconnected pieces with no insight into how they relate to one another, and Bazalgette (1992) points out that the categories in which media are placed influence how those texts are interpreted. I found evidence of these two phenomena when one teacher told me that he had his middle school students (ages 11–13) read Bigelow's (1995) cultural critique of *Oregon Trail II*. This article points out many of the problems of representation inherent in the software that I have mentioned above. After reading the article, the middle school students felt that Bigelow had really missed the mark. After all, they said, 'It's just a game. It doesn't teach us anything.' Although these students had learned about this historical period in their previous studies of material presented in various media, they had not independently made connections among the multiple ways in which the content was presented. The fact that they had categorized the software as a game further prohibited them from making content connections. They experienced *Oregon Trail II* in relation to their previous experiences with video games. They used their prior knowledge of the conventions of video games when making decisions concerning their travel, rather than their prior knowledge of life on the Trail and wilderness survival techniques. As Barthes (1974) notes, the meaning of the text is created by the intellectual links made by the reader. Thus readers experience each new text in terms of their experiences with previous texts. These students were presented with the simulation as a free-time game, disconnected from their study of the historical period which occurred in their previous years of schooling. The unguided ways in which these students had experienced *Oregon Trail II* before reading Bigelow's critique created the context for construing the simulation as a game, as something that wasn't meant to teach them anything. It is interesting to note that these students had all been identified as gifted, so it seems that even the brightest students need guidance in ways to read multiple texts and how to make meaningful connections among them.

Both my own playing of *Oregon Trail II,* and the response of the middle school students to Bigelow's cultural critique, reminded me of the complexities in studying history. Understanding social, political and economic relationships helps to make history richer. *Oregon Trail II* is devoid of features that could have brought embedded assumptions and understandings to my attention. It was only my deeper knowledge of the time period that enabled me to contextualize the software. Without conscious links to other texts about the American Westward Movement, the program offers little in helping players understand the circumstances of the times. And, without conscious links to present-day decision-making situations and the repercussions of those decisions, the program offers little in helping players transfer decision-making in a simulated environment to decision-making in real life.

WHAT WE LEARNED

This recategorization of console games as literature has enabled us to better understand them as texts worth reading. We can now see how these games, and even their more combat-focused counterparts, represent the changing nature of narrative. To varying degrees, each of these texts drew us into its story world (Langer, 1992). Once there, we each experienced thoughts and emotions evoked by the interplay of the text with our personal backgrounds and understandings. We were immersed in an alternate reality that is the hallmark of a literary experience. We brought to bear our existing interpretive abilities as experienced readers of literature and found that we were able to make rich meaning. By focusing on our own responses to these games, we were better able to value and interpret them as texts that enable us to learn about ourselves and society. We also realized that console games rely on, and extend how we define and experience narrative (Murray, 1997) in terms of plot, agency, positionality and conventions.

First, we came to better understand different ways that plot can unfold in this new environment. Console game narratives are more of a mosaic than a linear recounting of time-ordered events. They can be more circular and recursive than print narratives have traditionally been (Buckingham and Sefton-Green, 1994). Many modern and contemporary writers, from James Joyce to William Faulkner to Toni Morrison, have experimented with offering multiple viewpoints and fracturing the notion of continuous time. Computer technology builds on and offers a range of media that enhances these ways of representing experience. Meaning is constructed more from a juxtaposition of different texts rather than from extrapolation of the significance of events and characters, as is the case in more linear narratives. Consideration of multiple points of view is central to interpretation, a way to represent both a shared reality and individual experiences. For example, the plot of *Riven* becomes richer upon consulting the print documents included in, and accompanying, the visual and aural images. The various locker and faculty icons in *Rockett's New School* enable players to make decisions by putting together information gathered through encountering students and reading the way they look, descriptions of their personalities, contents of student lockers and per-spectives of teachers. It is through reading across and among these various media that events unfold.

Second, we learned that console games can allow for an increased sense of agency over paper-print narratives. 'Agency is the satisfying power to take meaningful action and see the results of our decisions and choices. We expect to feel agency on the computer when we double-click on a file and see it open before us or when we enter numbers in a spreadsheet and see the totals readjust. However, we do not usually expect to experience agency within a narrative environment' (Murray, 1997, p. 126). In other words, when we read novels, our response is governed primarily by identification with an already constructed character or situation. We do not expect to have any impact on the characters or environment. However, since computer narratives allow for an increased measure of physical control over the events in the unfolding narrative, the line between author and reader of print narrative is blurred, with the player actually authoring events within the rule-governed world of the game. Many different narratives can be constructed by the same or different players. This more open narrative framework can create a wider field of play than print can accommodate, a place where multiple alternatives, rather than identification, work to immerse us in the text. Closure or satisfaction with response may come more from exhaustion of possibilities than from arriving at a conclusion. Again, as with plot, the degree of agency is controlled by the sophistication of the game itself. In terms of the games we played, we would consider *Riven* to provide the greatest sense of agency and *Rockett's New School* to offer the least, with *Oregon Trail* somewhere in between the other two.

Third, let us consider positionality. As readers, we are familiar with how print text usually positions us by controlling the point of view of the narrator or narrators. In a similar fashion, console games also position the player. A player can be positioned as an omniscient viewer of the action as it unfolds on the screen, much as we are when we view most television programmes. Or, a player can be positioned right behind the character he or she is controlling, able to share their viewpoint, as well as see the character in action. And, as in paper-print narratives, the player's position can be shifted for different purposes within the game, as Leslie described in her account of *Oregon Trail*. However, console games can successfully position players in ways that are difficult to achieve in print. A player can be positioned *as* a character with the ability to move, pick things up, push buttons, and generally act on the environment without being able to see the character's body. This position generally corresponds to paper-print narratives written in the second person, but, as Penny experienced in *Riven*, the computer has the capability of making this position more engaging, of actually placing the reader in the story world as a character. In virtual reality systems, where console games will eventually evolve, players are positioned as characters and can see evidence of their physical being, such as the hand that pushes the button or the wings that propel them as they fly.

Fourth, we had to extend our repertoire of strategies for working within the conventions of this new genre. Across all three games we had to learn the conventions of movement and what different icons meant. As with any new genre, conventions for texts have not been stabilized, and given the rate at which computer technology progresses, may never be stabilized enough to make their way into the school curriculum. Game developers have addressed this by making the most of the more general conventions for play explicit in accompanying materials, as in *Riven*, or by simplifying the game, as in *Rockett's New School*. This allows them to develop conventions for navigating space and time tailored to a particular environment and to experiment freely with new representations of events and characters.

Finally, and probably most importantly, we learned that, in spite of what students said in the classroom that Leslie described earlier, these games can, and most likely do, teach something. It is to a discussion of teaching and learning in relationship to these new works of literature that we now turn.

SOME IMPLICATIONS FOR TEACHING

We believe that teachers need to become familiar with console games and explore their own responses to them. We cannot pretend that console games are going to go away and that we, as teachers, can make them go away by instilling a love of paper-print narratives. As the young man at the beginning of this article states, these new texts are too powerfully immersive and offer players many of the same emotional benefits as reading literature. Our students are unlikely to put them down and run for the library. We also cannot assume that console games inspire only mindless finger twitching. Even in most combat games there is an element of strategy and, in some of the newer games, an element of character interpretation – most combatants have their own styles of fighting and players can select the style with which they feel most comfortable.

We consider console games as texts worth serious consideration in classrooms. In media studies such serious consideration takes the form of, for example, investigations of the origin of these texts; analyses of the audiences they were intended for and appeal to; study of how the codes and language of different media contribute to meaning; research on how consumers categorize and respond to different texts within and across categories; and critique of implicit social, political and economic messages embedded within these texts (Bazalgette, 1992). These activities are worth pursuing. However, we believe that an exploration of students' experiences as players is a necessary precursor to these more analytic pursuits. Student and teacher responses can serve as data for an initial exploration of patterns of response that can lead to an ever-widening circle of analysis.

By thinking of these games as a form of narrative, we can use strategies from reader-response criticism to help our students to represent their experiences as players within these texts to learn about themselves, others, and the culture that produces and plays them. In other words, helping our students approach console games as literature may enhance the more analytic study typically found in media classrooms. By first studying our own diverse responses, we can ground our analyses in our own personal meanings, encouraging our students to question, revise and extend that meaning as they position themselves and their interpretations among the analytical frames provided by media studies.

In many English classrooms, we often focus on teaching the conventions of various kinds of texts; however, we can't even know all the conventions that they will need to understand them because, as we said earlier, they are constantly evolving. We need instead to create, with our students, a willingness to take risks and to experiment in an environment of shared inquiry. Study of console games offers an excellent opportunity for students and teachers to share expertise – with students offering their expertise in the playing of the game and teachers offering their expertise on making meaning with text. Bringing such texts into the classroom may also help to us to involve students in discussions of class, ethnic, racial and gender biases related to this genre of literature.

We can help students to understand the immersive, co-creative properties of console games and see them as metaphors for how to approach all texts with a stronger feeling of agency, equipping them with strategies that can make them better readers of their world. And, hopefully, the more circular and ambiguous nature of computer narratives can promote tolerance for ambiguity and difference, and enhance our abilities to live in an increasingly unpredictable and multicultural 'real' world.

NOTES

1   We use the term 'console games' (Sanger, 1997) as a general term that encompasses personal computer gaming software, playstation software, like those developed for Nintendo and Sony playstations, and games available on the Internet.
2   We use the term 'paper-print literature' rather than 'print literature' because many console games rely heavily on print.
3   See Sanger (1997) for a taxonomy of console games.
4   I originally intended to try *Myst* first, but I had difficulty locating an Apple Mac version of *Myst* in game stores, so I ended up buying the Fifth Anniversary Commemorative Edition. This edition allows you to send away for the Apple Mac version, which, at the time of this writing, had not arrived.

Chapter 7

Changing Technology, Changing Shakespeare, or Our Daughter is a Misprint

STEPHEN CLARKE

INTRODUCTION

When I wrote previously (Clarke, 1995) about the topic of Shakespeare and Information Technology (IT), I deliberately took the stance of advocating the use of the new technologies on the grounds that their inevitable employment in schools (and since 1995 their inevitability has taken clearer forms) would help dispel the notion of statutory formulas for the study of Shakespeare, canonically approved interpretations and centralist control over meanings. I was trying to combat some of the ill-derived certainty, as I saw it, of the then new National Curriculum, compulsory for virtually all schools in England and Wales (DFE, 1995), about set authors and the notion of literary heritage. The new National Curriculum (NC) had substituted compulsion via brief statements for the previous NC's tendency, for the subject English, to justify and explain a case (DES, 1990). I chose to argue by suggesting that the digitized images would give rise to comparative readings of the plays and an understanding of their cultural relativity in history rather than their fixed value in the stern and frozen eye of heritage. Since then, in our country, the centralists have changed their personnel a little, but not their instincts, and are now advocating and compelling ICT (Information and Communications Technology) use with a force previously reserved for selections from literature (DfEE, 1998).

During the same period that selected plays became the subjects of central direction and control, more plays than the set three at Key Stage 3[1] became the subjects of a renewed interest at the level of their provenance. Recent work (e.g. Sutherland, 1997) on the contribution of electronic images to the process of editing literary texts has emphasized, not the pure or unalloyed blessing of the technology, but its highly significant role in certain capacities. For helping us to look at Shakespeare edition variants, the computer has great virtue as a means of allowing multiple yet close comparisons, but in terms of this chapter I note that at base and root of Shakespeare study are physical objects, things, printed texts, whose pages and words point to variety, multiplicity and critical engagement with uncertainty on the part of anyone taking them seriously. Simultaneous to the plays' elevation as objects of compelled value, the computer has enabled some of them to be seen, with a clarity not easily shared before, as uncertain, erroneous and relative in their most basic forms. It did not, of course, take a computer to restore our daughter's name's spelling to its original probable form, but I was reminded of the Oxford edition's adoption of 'Innogen' in reading Donaldson (1997).

When Shakespeare plays and ICT are compelled subjects in the curriculum it is time to weigh up how they might be reconciled by English teachers looking to accommodate yet more items in the scope of their teaching. Perhaps they can have not only a co-existence but a beneficial relationship to one another. They would be enjoying their relationship at a time when English mother-tongue speakers around the world are constantly performing and adapting the plays for local cultures. The Globe Theatre in London might serve, perhaps, as a reference point for historical and geographical rootedness, while in other directions and outside the UK entirely, differences in accent, humour and topicality are likely to grow and influence the teaching here, as with the Lurhman *Romeo & Juliet.*

In this chapter I have no wish to repeat the attempt to write from a combative stance so much as try to give a dispassionate evaluation of the potential for ICT to develop, extend and enrich the study of Shakespeare in schools. I suggest at the same time that the process is reciprocal, and that Shakespeare studies in English can help considerably in the construction of a solution to a large problem inherent within ICT in education, and for English especially, namely the evaluation, by students as they use it, of the 'information' element of ICT.

This chapter is structured on a simple two-fold division. I begin by exploring what the new technologies might add to the list of approaches to the study of the plays, assuming that an overview should try to bring together existing developments with further possibilities, and end by trying to show how, with a play as the imaginative centre, a series of texts may be assembled and constructed around it which encourage the comparative study of different media and text types, including the now necessary 'informational' texts. For the English teacher hard-pressed to find time in which to fit an increasing and increasingly diverse set of demands, the opportunities offered for deductive and critical cross-comparisons of documentary texts may enable the completion of one aim while pursuing another.

WHAT DIGITAL TECHNOLOGIES CAN ACHIEVE THAT OTHERS CANNOT

The computer allows us access to Shakespeare's plays, to multiple varieties of printed versions available previously only to scholars and at the same time, also on the computers, we have open, as never before, a rich set of possibilities for comparing performances of different plays which have been filmed or become the subjects of visual record in certain ways. If those two aspects of computer use are seen as too advanced, and some of them certainly would be for school students, then one other aspect remains vital, that of Shakespeare on the Web. Between these three – and the last is not definable in singular terms or category – the possibilities for involvement, discussion, exchange, rehearsal and enjoyment are real enough. None of them can hope to shift the teacher away from the challenging enterprise of having the play in hand, well performed by the class, but most forms of Shakespeare study involve sedentary activities too, such as solo or paired reading, talking, interpreting to oneself, studying and analysing films of performances and writing, and these need never be altogether disconnected from personal involvement in an actual class-based performance. In all of these, ICT might have an influence and a capacity to shape the forms of study.

We need, then, to try to list in some systematic way what the computer can achieve that may not have been readily possible before its arrival both in universities, where future teachers study, and in schools. It seems to me that in the fulfilment of a coherent interrelationship between Shakespeare in English and ICT, the technology and its associated systems have a part to play at four levels:

1. *Textual presentation*, which is very book-like, except that search facilities and electronic cross-comparisons can help the reader explore printed texts in ways which are simply unavailable from the book. If we consult, say, the work of Donaldson (*ibid.*), we see that the electronic presentation of images of printed pages of a play raises very interesting questions about how to read, study and compare.
2. *Textual realization*, which enables the idea of consulting small-screen versions (reductions?) of different productions, from film or television, in order to understand how 'the' idealized play is an abstract concept, compared with the more amenable idea of 'versions of a script'. Friedlander (1991) offers a fascinating account of easily observable differences between performances of five lines from *Hamlet*, and how these differences might set students thinking about that moment in the play. These differences, extracted from filmed versions of *Hamlet*, could easily enough, at the technical level, be juxtaposed on a circuit somewhere and made available to students.
3. *Textual change*, in which students can take the 'original' (or the nearest thing we have to it), or an existing interpretation, and alter it, play with the play with youthful disrespect and probably ignorance, but in doing so imitate their elders and betters, from Nahum Tate with his eighteenth-century ideas of an 'improved' ending for *King Lear*, suitable for the refined sensibilities of bourgeois London, to Tom Stoppard's dramatized thoughts on the nature of *Hamlet* in *Rosencrantz and Guildenstern Are Dead*. In making adaptations and modernizations our students should learn a great deal about the narrative, structure, tone and language of the play.

4. *Response to texts*, which refers to the technologies enabling students to pool and compare their thoughts and questions in ways which perhaps, on the evidence to date, are far from what we would wish them to be. 'Chat-line Shakespeare', only in written form, may not be what the National Grid for Learning, a political project in the UK for bringing schools the benefits of on-line access, quite has in mind, but the easily accessible evidence of response is there and may be illustrative of things we should bear in mind about the teaching.

PERFORMANCES AS DIGITIZED IMAGES

Already available and popularly used in the UK, probably at home as well as at school given their sales in computer warehouses, are the BBC Shakespeare CD-Roms of individual plays. I chose these as examples because they are conveniently available, although their equivalents exist in other countries. The structure of these discs is such that it permits an easy path between items, and in this alone encourages the reader or browser to explore without anxiety both the verbal text (the script) and the world created around the script. However, in part the mixed-media format assumes that we are able to absorb multiple messages. That we can watch actors and hear them speaking while listening to accompanying music is well evident, but if an entire portion of play script is added to one side of the screen and not just a few subtitled words of it, then the viewer/reader relationship is in danger of becoming slightly schizophrenic.

What the mixed-media device ought to allow, if used in the most thoughtful way, is a realization, by students, of the relationship of script to performance. I have, again, to rely very heavily on Donaldson for this idea, as for much else, but his account of comparative extracts from different filmed performances, able to be brought up on screen after a portion of the printed text has been highlighted, strikes me as exactly the kind of development of Shakespeare studies which ICT can best promote. We need, in this area as in others which preceded it, to examine how best to adapt, for school purposes and within a budget, the work of pioneer scholars in university English departments. One obvious limitation to the BBC CDs, understandable, however, given the copyright laws, is that the performances on video are all from the same production. In order to benefit from the technology's capacity to heighten their understanding of the power of a Shakespeare script, our students need to see, for example, drawn from Friedlander, the acutely different reactions of a number of Hamlets to their meeting with an equal and opposite number of Ophelias to see how ambiguous and open are the words:

Hamlet: Soft you now,
            The fair Ophelia. Nymph, in thy orisons
            Be all my sins remembered.

Ophelia: Good my lord,
            How does your honour for this many a day?

Shakespeare films (e.g. Reynolds, 1991 or Davies and Wells, 1994) need to be the subjects of fast and easy access in English classrooms in convenient forms. Enthusiastic teachers have long since compared different performances of the same moment on ordinary video, and they involve their students in analyses which differ in kind from the deployment of differently edited scripts to the psychology of character. ICT use could both spread, extend and deepen such comparative reading practices. Jacobi as Hamlet may be compared to Williamson, may be compared to Olivier, may be compared to the Hamlet actor in the Kosintzev film, Innokenti Smotounovski, may be compared to Mel Gibson, and so on, at key moments. Teachers would need to show that differences lie, not just in acting styles or verbal emphases, but in directorial decisions too, such as the inclusion of the larger world in the Kosintzev *Hamlet* and its near total exclusion from the Olivier film.

THE PRINTED PLAYS AS DIGITIZED IMAGES

We shall return to the business of using the technologies to help students discover access to the theatricality of the scripts which they study, but first we need to examine the capacity of the technology to uncover, at student level, the nature of the printed Shakespeare text. Imagine a student, who reaches university to study for an English degree, most of whose modules relate to the study of Literature. For this student, previous Shakespeare studies at school may well have been based around truly authoritative editions of a play or plays, but the teachers did not pause for long on the background to the actual text in hand, instead focusing on the background of the life and times, cultural, social and political, of Shakespeare and the look and dimensions of the theatres in which Shakespeare and his players worked. This work (in the 'sixth form' in the UK) had been decidedly helpful in allowing our student to contextualize and redefine some of the previously slightly hazy ideas about who Shakespeare was, but the text itself had been treated with some reverence, sometimes given over to minute study and analysis which had the virtue of developing the subtlety of critical thought. Between the printed text and response there was at times a teacher, at times not, but the studying had had to proceed on the assumption that the text, or at any rate individual words within it, was or were what Shakespeare himself wrote. The printed text was the authoritative text, whether on paper or screen, on its own or accompanied by other images.

The student discovers, however, that one mark of transition between school and university relates precisely to the provenance of the play texts. At university our student probably encounters a much more systematic study of the way in which the plays were printed, discovering in the process which plays are relatively secure, as editions, and which insecure, and it comes as something of a surprise to our student to discover that corrections were inserted between copies of the same print-run. How could these people have been so careless, he or she wonders? But this curiosity is real enough, and in part because the evidence is present in virtual form. Donaldson (*ibid.*) shows us, through a few reproduced images, how the first page of *The Tempest* can be presented on screen so that comparison may be made between pages which were presumably intended to be identical, but which are different, to greater or lesser degrees.

In engaging for a while with the images on screen, the student is going beyond simple background study and into the world of editing – the world previously reserved for scholars who might gain access to precious copies or facsimiles of them, but who were able to do so through their status and acknowledged expertise. That the first-year undergraduates step into the role of scholars is a change in custom allowed by the power of the programs which run the images of the texts together in certain illuminating ways. It should occasion no surprise, nor does it, I think, that the novices should be brought up against realms of difficulty previously kept beyond their invitation. The same movement from simple repetition of safe and received opinions about texts, to personal and demanding encounters with them, and with their difficulties and ambiguities happened, historically, about seventy or eighty years ago, or earlier, both by Dixon's (1991) account and Shayer's (1972). Perhaps the significant point to stress in this area is that the computer also allows a regular comparison of the original printed version(s) and a modern re-spelled and edited authoritative text, and in these comparisons all kinds of differences can be systematically noted and explored. What the computer gives to the exercise is a single medium which enables readers to perceive differences readily and note them by cutting, pasting and adding their own commentaries. Advanced students could note how spelling has changed, or punctuation, or, quite differently, media studies students could use such textual comparisons to note the power of printers and editors to mediate and regularize a (sadly invisible) product.

THE SPEECH AND LANGUAGE OF THE PLAYS IN DIGITAL FORM

In noting how the new technologies have brought about this kind of change, or potential change, I am reminded of Lanham's thesis (1993) to the effect that changing technologies will change disciplines. One example provided by Lanham relates to the study, not of Shakespeare, but of Chaucer. Think, he says, about how students might learn to read a Chaucer poem from a computer with the sound of the poem, properly read, in an accent of the time of the writing accompanying the scrolling words. Such isolated and computer-based study would enable students to control the speed of scrolling and extent of text revealed, and make it their business to read along with the voice-over, and thus to enact, however quietly and privately, a performance of the poem.

This change from traditional classroom-based instruction with a group to computer-based solo work might be usable with Shakespeare texts, or at any rate with portions of a play. There is abundant evidence in, for example, *The Dillen* (Hewins, 1981) of how Shakespeare productions became, in the later nineteenth and earlier twentieth centuries, associated with the accents and pronunciations of the cultured upper-middle class. It is hard to imagine the same accents applying, say, to pre-Establishment productions, such as, to take a fictional example, the *Hamlet* of Mr Wopsle narrated in great satiric detail in *Great Expectations*. In Dickens, incidentally, Shakespeare and anarchy go together.

But to return to the question of which kind of accent has been granted the lease on Shakespeare performance in approved and well-funded centres we note that the 'accents yet unknown' was a remarkable prophecy in *Julius Caesar*. The well-structured CD-Rom could easily enough, at a technical level, demonstrate how a well-known speech might sound in the accent of Shakespeare's time, and at different moments since. There is some attention to this on the existing discs, but more remains to be done, I think, with demonstrations of not only an 'original' accent, but regional varieties from existing sets, such as the opening of *Richard III* in the way spoken by Rutter's company, The Northern Drift, which illustrates that those lines would appear to have been written for a northerner:

Now is the winter of our discontent
Made glorious summer by this son of York.

There are some twenty or twenty-two syllables in the opening two lines (depending on how many you count 'our' and 'glorious' as having), and yet no fewer than eight of them are susceptible to a distinctly northern pronunciation; the main verb and first-word-of-line stress falls noticeably on one of them. The effect is to shake previous expectations, based around Olivier's performance in the film of 1955. That extract too could be on a CD-Rom. Examining differences of this kind would do little, perhaps, to change one's view of the character of the protagonist, unless it is that the regional emphasis suggests a man less likely to be a national king than a local baron, but the very act of re-casting the accent and the expectations which accompany it is in line with Tony Harrison's idea of taking right and valued pronunciation out of the hands of the receivers. Some computers allow their users to create CD-Roms, so, equipped with one, pupils might create accented readings, and might well enjoy a 'karaoke' approach, dubbing their own accents to fit the mouth-movements of, say, Olivier. Thus might northern students, or those with accents originated in the colonies, witness their variants gain a little brief authority.

What is at issue is the use to which the performed text has been put over the course of a history of appropriation. If written text became the property of the academy and rich libraries, the performed text was looked after by self-appointed guardians from a social class that wished to distinguish itself by, among other features, speech. That social class linked its own speech, through, one could argue, patronage to culturally revered texts, and all kinds of evidence about relationships between character, style of speaking, accent used, provenance of performance and context of performance could be placed on a single CD-Rom. Such comparative studies of accents at work ought to be at least as interesting as looking at differences in the costumes of *Macbeth*. This latter study, enabled on the BBC CD-Rom, is a powerful one for seeing how ideologies and fashions have had their influences at different historical moments, but clothing is not the only vehicle for that.

LEARNING TO READ THE DIGITIZED IMAGES

Donaldson, though, has another and, to me, more significant idea to explore which bears very closely upon concepts which are at the heart of the complexities of interweaving English and ICT. The area concerned is the question of how different media and different kinds of text permit, encourage or enforce different kinds of reading. The context for this discussion is the question of how it is that we could read variants of words or lines where there is divergent evidence about what should count as authentic, but that, on the single printed page of a book we very often do not. Logically there is nothing to stop us doing so if the variant word is available as a footnote, but something about our accustomed behaviour as readers of a page makes us most reluctant to go looking for differences to what we have just made perfect sense of, or, if the passage is difficult, of what we have just struggled to make satisfactory sense of. As Donaldson puts it (p. 187): '. . . knowledge of variation, even the highly selected knowledge presented in the textual notes of a typical edition, is theoretical rather than active'.

When different facsimile pages are available for inspection on a single screen, to the general reader as if to an editor, then looking at originals and beginning to study them closely invites close comparison; we go looking for inconsistencies between variants of the same page as if in that detective-work lay the reward for our pains. The theory of being interested in variance, usually a low level of interest for even the advanced-level school student, may stand a good chance of being transformed into practice. The average English student, however, if engaged on this activity, might enjoy other readerly pleasures located in the facsimiles, such as the surprise of seeing for the first time the original spellings, 'Bote' for 'Boat', as in 'Bote-swaine' for example, from the First Folio of *The Tempest*.

Reading from the screen would be hard to sustain if we are trying to read the play as a dramatic and fulfilling experience, turning the words into drama on the stage of our own minds, but examining even a little of a carefully arranged selection of facsimile pages could help students to make two important observations. The first is that there is a lack of manuscript; from the start it is entirely possible that other hands adapted an original. The second is that the modern and approved books we use are themselves interpretations – a chosen set of words from a possible set. Between these two the students might see that although each play is limited in scope (and meaning), the very provisionality suggests a greater care for the right performance than the right poem. These points have been made repeatedly in discourse about teaching Shakespeare, but the technologies allow us to ground the theories. No longer need Quartos and Folios be part of an arcane language. A good way of getting students to select and highlight their perceptions of differences between editions would be via the power-point presentation mechanism, where information is dynamically ordered and presented. Behind all such work the English teacher ought, I believe, to introduce an element of reflection on the act of writing the Shakespeare play. The manuscript may have been in one hand only, or it may have been by one hand predominantly with the interpolations of others. When handwriting changed to print, on what or whose authority did the original printers act? Questions should be set about who and what the handwriting or printing was for. The needs of printers would not have been primary needs, perhaps, as Shakespeare wrote, but would the same be true for a playwright today? We could begin some thinking about how production technologies and writing technologies have changed, and how their relationship to one another has also changed.

LEARNING TO WRITE THE DIGITIZED IMAGES

It should be a relatively easy step for someone concerned to bring to Shakespeare studies a significant degree of evidence about how 'Shakespeare' has been defined, used, exploited, honoured, adapted and transformed, to juxtapose sets of images and words so that lines of changing thought may be perceived; but more than just perceived. At some point we should invite the students to see themselves as heirs to the process of interpretation and transformation. The PCs of the very late twentieth century probably contain sufficient memory and storage power to act as devices whereby groups of students can begin to think of themselves as directors of a play. Friedlander's chapter is fascinating about the capacity of certain programs, specially constructed for his own pioneering teaching, to encourage students unused to thinking about the staging and theatricality of the plays to begin exploring dimensions, appearances, space, gesture and action as items created on a screen. Similar work is routine in other media, but computers can combine media for creative purposes as well as for presentational purposes. No doubt aspects of the final products would appear pre-cast or stereotyped, but imagine the fun of animating illustrations of an Edmund Kean or Beerbohm Tree, with the aim of rendering other quite different poses to the givens which are familiar but static moments from a dynamic. Add to the new poses (and marks will be awarded for stylistic consistency with the originals) lines or words as uttered during that sweep of the arm or turn of the head, either as printed subtitles or dubbed voices of the students.

In these kinds of activity, which I believe to be perfectly, technically feasible, we can see the beginnings of the ways in which study and action can be fruitfully inter-related. Rehearsing the lines to work well with the animated and transformed images may well bring English, drama, computer-studies, graphic art even, and music together, as indeed they function in harmony on stage. In the UK we had the good luck, in the 1980s, to have the Shakespeare Project, directed by Rex Gibson, re-invigorate teaching methods for use with school students of a wide range of ages. One brief space later we need the same optimism, energy and belief to be put into a project for exploiting the potential of the new technologies for supporting the teaching of Shakespeare. The methodologies and approaches advocated and instanced in the Shakespeare in Schools project should be the basis of future work, and anything which the technologies can add should be in line with the liveliness, irreverence and careful balance between text-centredness and student-centredness which that project achieved.

HOW SHAKESPEARE STUDIES MIGHT PUT ICT INTO CRITICAL PERSPECTIVE

The familiar image of the Shakespeare head, re-fashioned as Will the cool dude which heads up the Lurhman *Romeo & Juliet* website serves as a convenient example of Shakespeare re-appropriated. It happens to be, I think, just one in a series of re-appropriations of one Shakespeare portrait over a period of hundreds of years; it is also in line with many other commercially intended acts of irreverence to the icons, such as Michelangelo's 'David' photographed in cut-off Levis. The computer would allow a convenient juxtaposition, and thus comparison, between the portrait and its parody. Both could, in class, be printed and presented to pairs of pupils who are asked to write explanatory notes on the connotations of each portrait, or do so on screen. I've no doubt that this has been done, but I advocate this kind of comparative activity as a model for other aspects of textual study and evaluative thinking. It may be media study more than part of literary study, but that is where the multi-media machinery is pushing the subject English. English, though, can push back and a creative dialogue develop. Students bring quantities of more or less explicit knowledge of media to school with them, and engagements of the kind advocated here help to refine and develop that media knowledge.

Few other kinds of literary engagements are quite so deep in performance records, or lend themselves quite so well to a study of historical change, as do Shakespeare's plays. In looking, in addition to their own rehearsals and part performances, at variant drafts of the plays, at enacted scenes from theatre, film and video, and at such popular items as the Animated Tales, at later changes in wording, and at conventional copies of the play with good supporting notes, photographs and questions, the school students are learning exactly what is required of them in their National Curriculum (DFE, 1995). In that document, pupils in English are required, under the heading 'Reading', to 'compare and synthesise information drawn from different texts, e.g. *IT-based sources and printed articles*'. That comparison could not only apply to the kinds of text listed above, but to texts additional to the play text and performance; the comparative evaluation of different programmes and posters, critical accounts of performances and powerful images could be also structured around the documentation surrounding productions, ephemeral perhaps, but comparable and genre-specific ephemera nevertheless.

Thoughtful use of ICT, as IT has now been summarily re-named in the UK, depends upon comparisons. I have no quarrel with that idea. In Shakespeare study terms, we note that there are likely to be very easily available comparisons ready to be constructed, perhaps at first by teachers, but with the students taking over as they catch on to the nature of the game, and play yet further games with the play they started with. A succession of texts to compare could be assembled, starting with single pictures and progressing, say, to sophisticated reviews of differences between two performances of *Hamlet*. The reviews could be written by a student or found from a search in printed newspapers or those held on the Web, or a CD-Rom. If they were professional, printed reviews, then they might be more in line with a received definition of 'information' than the student compositions. As such, their value would lie in their susceptibility to, not just content analysis (how each evaluated the performance seen), but to an analysis of their characteristic styles and linguistic conventions.

In addition to learning to distinguish between print sources and digitally held sources the student would learn to theorize, however tentatively and as an initiate, about a wide range of text types. This could happen with a Shakespeare play as the centre and its enactments as the study of textual differences and conventions. Filmed *Macbeth*s have differences between one another, but they have similarities, perhaps, which are not shared at all with televised *Macbeth*s.

Within the scope of this activity the student becomes able to develop sufficient and naturally growing familiarity with a range of text types. From familiarity might grow, with the right prompts, curiosity about aspects of this range. The technology differentiates and sub-divides in its own ways, but for the student there is every need to see connections between items located, not merely in different places, but under quite different kinds of heading. However, in bringing this clarity and comparative thinking about, the technology can act as a considerable help. Once ascended, the ladder can be thrown down, and so, at the final point of comparative thought, stand images and experiences of the play which owe nothing at all to digital technology but which were refined and clarified against other images in ICT's use.

For example, a chart could be devised, on a database, which listed some key differentiators such as enjoyment, extent of original script used within a delimited portion of filmed text chosen by the teacher, style indicators, accent variation, effects of the medium, date produced, and so on. The finished product, put together on screen but also available as a print text, would consist of a series of findings such as that the best Macbeth actor seen was McKellen on a video of a television broadcast based on an RSC production (with a still photograph from a video whose choice had occasioned much debate), that the most enjoyable activity was acting out the murder of Lady Macduff's children (again with still photograph, this time from the class video of this scene), that the most silly image of Macbeth from a large number of candidates was that showing him as a Viking, found on the CD-Rom (and reproduced), that the following images contain their own clues about how they are constructed for audiences who were (i) Japanese, (ii) seated in front of a television, (iii) in the cinema and (iv) in the theatre, and that, finally for this list, the strangest re-writing of the script belonged to Edwin Morgan (passage duly reproduced, inviting viewers to chance their mimicking powers into the computer's microphone).

In all these kinds of reading of images could lie, if well developed through teaching, a better understanding of 'text' in its possible and necessary variant forms, than the simplified book-of-the-play to be read aloud in class that occasioned me so much pleasure while at school. Ours was a lively and engaging methodology for the late 1950s and early 1960s, but 40 years on and one entire revolution later (the forecast of whose arrival I remember reading about in the school library), we need something more in line with contemporary abilities and inclinations.

NOTE

1   Key Stage (KS) 3 denotes the ages 11–14, and the Shakespeare play studied for the English test for 14-year-olds at the end of the Key Stage must be one of: *A Midsummer Night's Dream*, *Julius Caesar* or *Romeo and Juliet*, at the time of going to press.

Chapter 8

Texting: Reading and Writing in the Intertext

ANDREW GOODWYN

This chapter examines the fundamental relationship between reading and writing and contextualizes it within the emerging, and by no means stable, world of the electronic media. It begins with some examples of current, and in the best sense traditional, practice, considers how these are presently evolving and offers some views on how these practices may develop in the next decade. This chapter concentrates initially on the potential of the word processor, then attempts to place the convergence of media and computer technologies at the centre of English as a site for intensive and powerful analysis and creativity. In order to achieve this it examines the issues of presentation, representation and of how students can reach much higher levels of engagement by treating electronic texts as dynamic and malleable, offering every reader the opportunity to become that text's writer; students become what I playfully call 'textists'. It considers the roles of teachers and students as symbolic analysts and symbolic artists. These somewhat off-putting terms are explained and, I hope, made user friendly. This chapter tries to illustrate how we can make the maximum use of the current capabilities of the convergence of Information and Communication Technologies with media technologies and offers some cautions and some optimistic visions of the decidedly imminent future.

GOOD PRESENTATION?

Within the English curriculum, certainly in the UK, the most frequent current application of the computer is as a word processor. The research evidence we have shows that the majority of such work is in the category of presentation (Goodwyn, 1997). Typically, children will have worked in their classrooms, possibly for some time, on producing a handwritten text and then they enter the computer environment to create a 'final' version. In some cases this may still be within the well-established tradition of 'writing up for best', which is the equivalent of producing a final, exceptionally neat, handwritten copy. It is certainly true that for some teachers this is already an opportunity to go further. For example, a poem, rather than simply being typed up, can be more carefully spaced, the lines can be more precisely adjusted and the poet can select a font to embody the tone or theme of the work. This approach marks a minimal move from merely re-presenting the text to beginning to represent the text. There are examples of much more imaginative approaches and I will consider those later in the chapter.

The key point at this stage is to examine how presentation can move to representation and this is not just re-presentation. Presentation can be defined as the way in which a completed text/image is finished so as best to present itself to its intended audience. Therefore any act of presentation contains within it an implicit act of representation: we set out handwritten poems differently to stories, we draw sketches in order, potentially, to create a picture. These acts are normalized within current creative practices and are used and taught in schools. Representation is essentially a much more powerful, meaning-making activity, when the creator of the text is able to consider a range of means for communicating the full potential of a text and has access to a repertoire of cultural resources.

My main argument in this chapter is that we have always lived in representational communities but that a convergence of technologies increasingly puts more and more people in control of representational resources. In other words, we can all take our 'normal' concern with presentation a step further and become more fully engaged with a deeper set of meanings. The role of schools and teachers is potentially enormous in developing and enhancing this capability. Although the home for many children (and adults) is becoming a far more dynamic environment for entertainment and information it will, in my view, retain its limitations as a place for social and collaborative learning. However wonderful or effective parent figures may be, they are not professional teachers and schools will retain a central role in organizing and facilitating learning environments that provide equal opportunities for all children.

To return to the concept of representation, good presentation has always been constructed as very important and one key role of schooling has been seen as the production of citizens who are presentable in the world, particularly of work. Hence, knowing how to behave and also knowing how to present oneself in written form are closely linked. The British obsession with school uniform has a direct bearing here: schools represent their effectiveness through an encompassing visible symbol that demands uniform good presentation for all their students. The current trend in the well-paid workplace appears to be moving in the opposite direction towards a more individual and relaxed mode of dress and towards the increasing opportunity for workers to use their own domestic environment for some of their work; this is one very obvious outcome of principally computer and telephone technologies. Workers in fast food and similar chains all have to wear uniform for similar reasons to school because this symbolizes that the management are in control and that uniform standards are in place. The trend towards individual choice for the most highly valued workers, I suggest, will steadily influence schools but in the short term it will make the concern with school uniformity even more pronounced.

Our concern here is with the other very visible form of good presentation and the renewed emphasis on good handwriting. Recent revisions to the National Curriculum in England and Wales have placed much greater emphasis on helping children to write legibly and fluently. In itself this is a perfectly acceptable and welcome emphasis and may be more enlightened than it appears. There is also plenty of research evidence (Smith, 1982 offers a good overview) supporting the idea that physically shaping and forming letters is educative and helps children to acquire the written symbol system of their language.

However, in the computer age there is a genuine probability that many children will find handwriting far less important to them than in the past, as will most adults. It is a technology of writing that will absolutely retain an importance although its relative importance in the most technologically advanced societies is already evidently greatly diminished. No teacher, however suspicious of the claims about computers as tools for education, can doubt the evidence of the world they now live in. A handwritten communication is increasingly rare in the adult world, in fact increasingly unacceptable; the only place dominated by handwriting is school. This is a genuinely awkward period of transition and, for primary teachers in particular, a quite unfair burden. They are charged with ensuring that all children by age 7 (in the UK) should:

hold a pencil comfortably in order to develop a legible style that follows the conventions of written English, including:

- writing from left to right and from the top to bottom of the page;
- starting and finishing letters correctly;
- regularity of size and shape of letter;
- regularity of spacing of letters and words.

They should be taught the conventional ways of forming letters, both lower case and capitals. They should build on their knowledge of letter formation to joining letters and words. They should develop an awareness of the importance of clear and neat presentation in order to communicate their meaning effectively. (DFE, 1995, p. 10)

The only reference to writing using a computer is the single phrase, 'Pupils should have opportunities to plan and review their writing, assembling and developing their ideas on paper and on screen' (*ibid.*, p. 9).

Whilst this demand is being made, and schools made publicly accountable for it, particularly in the UK through competitive league tables, teachers are faced with the irony that many of the most motivated children are writing at home on their computer and either using a keyboard or a mouse as the base for their communicative and creative functions. Schools in a very few years will have to adjust, and after the current apparently global upgrading of many school computer systems this dilemma will need a resolution. The likely outcome is that keyboarding and mouse (or whatever is used by then) manipulation skills will be taught in school as part of early literacy education.

Children will also, where relevant, be able to speak into their computer and it will create a text version for them. Teachers will immediately see positive and negative potential in this new form of talk-writing but this chapter will not devote space to this, as yet untried, in classroom terms, phenomenon. To sum up so far, children and their teachers will increasingly have a range of presentational/representational tools to select from and this will create new emphases and new dynamics for readers and writers.

UP CLOSE AND PERSONAL

My own view is that personal writing, which I am defining as writing by an individual, almost certainly to another important individual, written by hand, will take on a very special status. It will retain that unique signature quality that already marks its legal and personal qualities. In the adult world its precious, as in rare and highly valued, quality is likely to become even more visible. For example, in the most technological societies we continue to invent more and more occasions on which to give each other cards. Although there is undeniably a powerful commercial, profit-driven base to the manufacturing of some of these occasions, yet there is also an equally powerful human need at work to express love for others and to honour the place of key relationships. The cards themselves are usually made by machines and come with an acceptable, ritualized text, ironically personalized already ('Happy Birthday Uncle' and so on); the key element is the space left for the giver to add the genuine personal touch through personal writing and signature. Of course for the well-off these cards are already available as 'hand made' and are satisfyingly expensive, providing an extra level of the pseudo-personal to the giver and the recipient.

I think this point about the future of personal writing is highly significant and my example of cards has far more than merely illustrative value. For example, in British primary schools, many children are given curriculum time to produce cards to take home, despite the huge pressure induced by the combined weight of a National Curriculum, the Literacy Hour and the imminent Numeracy Hour (see Chapter 1 for reference to these govern-mental prescriptions). This is both a simple and personal task for each child and a complex occasion for the teacher. How do you mark, for example, the peculiarly Christian festival of Easter in a multicultural society? Or Mother's Day in a society where families contain mothers with a multiplicity of roles, one of which may well include a step-mother? These are not new demands but technological, media-saturated societies find it much harder to ignore their visibly changing social and cultural structures. The key point is that the personal, in this case the individual written artefact, takes on increased significance in a technological environment.

However, the obsession with handwriting must also be faced as just that: an obsession, rather tinged with nostalgia. Future students, while recognizing the value of the personal signature, will also have a much more varied repertoire of means to express the personal. All students need help and encouragement to become effective users of the pen; the same is even more true of, say, the pencil or the brush as used in art. However, no education system claims to turn out all future citizens who are uniformly effective artists. Handwriting is a prison for many students and adults.

Much energy has been spent on trying to develop a handwriting system that will enable everyone to have neat, legible and fluent handwriting. So far, human beings and handwriting are an indifferent combination, and a hundred years or so of compulsory education in the UK suggests that we are never going to attain a consistent level of competence. Expressed crudely, almost all writers can be legible, but for some this is at the expense of fluency and speed. The technology of the pen suits some people, the technology of the keyboard suits others better; this does not make handwriting redundant and never will. There is also a simple and fundamental point that pen technology is cheap and reliable, requires no 'peripherals' (batteries/power sources) and is far more portable than any current portable computer. Whatever the advances in technology, enabling incremental miniaturization and processing power, the above points about pen technology will remain important.

One ambiguous effect of the keyboard is an apparent removal of the personal identity of the writer as presented in the script; there is also a highlighting of the individuality of the writer by placing the reader's full attention on the text and its message. This is a half truth where the computer is concerned as the writer has an enormous scope to shape and reshape the text and experiment with presentation/representation. However, a very simple and important bonus of the computer is that many writers are released from the imprisonment of their own handwriting. Research (Goodwyn, 1997) shows that for many English teachers this is a recognized benefit, especially in motivating boys. This is an important benefit but it can be seen very much as a first stage.

Once such motivation is established then it should be possible to move to the second stage, where students can take increasing control over higher level textual strategies involving structures and cohesion, leading to an under-standing of the representational power of texts; this is the point at which presentation becomes both a powerful and a truly creative function. Most home computers, for example, already allow their users to create cards and calendars as personalized gifts. Whilst making no extravagant claims for this function it nevertheless illustrates the point at which technology places the individual in an active relationship to cultural resources that can be lovingly and thoughtfully personalized; this is certainly a development going a step beyond picking the 'right' card off the shelf. It is no coincidence that one can now pick electronic cards from the Internet and send them with a 'personalized', often multi-media, message. The concept of what is personal in sending and receiving messages is partly challenged and partly redefined in an electronic and media age. For teachers, especially those concerned as English teachers are with the personal, the individual, and the whole idea of the communicating self, the crucial concept is representation; for example, how does one represent oneself and one's feelings and concerns when everyone's 'personalized' message looks, apparently, the same?

REPRESENTATION IN THE SCHOOLING SYSTEM

In schools in England and Wales the issue of representation is certainly considered in many subjects. Within the artistic domain, Art and Drama frequently focus on this concept; Geography and History have their own concerns with culture and iconography; Languages, Science and Mathematics all introduce new elements of representation such as linguistic symbols, equations and mathematical symbols respectively. Examined from this perspective, the school curriculum is a highly wrought symbolic system suffused with representation. However, this is not how it is taught; attention to symbolic representation comes typically as content, with each subject attempting to ensure that students can handle its particular system. Numerical symbols are 'taught', for example, in Mathematics but relied on heavily in Science. There is, however, a pressure from within schools and from external sources to make teaching more concerned with representation. This is hardly surprising as a combination of factors make the lived world an environment increasingly suffused with representations and with a consciousness of these representations.

I would argue that Media Studies and Media Education are, as relatively new subjects in some English-speaking countries, the two areas where representation is a constant and crucial concept. I will refer to these as distinct subjects because, within the UK context, Media Studies has emerged as a specialist subject which students opt for at 14, 16, or in Higher Education, whereas Media Education can be found in various other subjects but principally in English teaching (Goodwyn, 1992, 1998). The subject owes much to its predecessors such as Sociology but it has, in the last fifteen years, come into its own. Our interest in this book lies not in the emergence of Media Studies *per se*, but in the convergence between the concepts crucial in that domain and in the ICT field.

I have touched in my opening chapter (Chapter 1) on how the original conception of the National Curriculum for English in England and Wales 'lumped' Media Education and Information Technology (IT) together. This was essentially a pragmatic action. These were two new areas in 1988 and as they were both somewhat technical in orientation and future-focused they had enough in common for an attempt to combine them in the same chapter. Since then, IT has become ICT, and a series of technical innovations such as satellite communication and digitization, combined with the enormous increase in the memory and processing speed of personal computers with access to the Internet, has meant that the computer has, essentially, entered the media domain. For example, one of the simplest but most profound results of the development of the Internet has been to make the computer screen a site of both symbolic analysis and creative interaction; I will return to this theme.

The convergence of technologies has profound implications for teachers of language and literature. It is important to recognize that other specialist teachers will have their own subject domains invigorated and redefined by the learning potential of the new technologies. A subject like Art, for example, can exploit vast high quality visual resources through CD-Roms and the Internet and can use the power of computers to allow students to interact with these resources from simply reading and analysing them, to making them into a part of their own artistic productions. However, the longer-term and more profound implications for English will be discussed in the final section of this chapter; at this point I need to return to the present and short-term future.

FROM TYPING TO TYPOGRAPHY

Typography was once, quite rightly, the specialist province of printers and publishers, people who physically constructed books. For centuries the author hand-wrote and then handed over the manuscript. Gradually, in this century, the writer offered a typescript and in the last decade it has become normal to hand over both hard copy and computer discs; relatively soon the author will simply send the text electronically and the publisher will convert it into various forms, one of which will be book form but other forms will multiply. Authors in the past principally wrote a text, without very much say in the design of the printed book. There have always been illustrated texts, and well-established authors such as the Dickenses and Thackerays of the nineteenth century certainly influenced the use and positioning of illustrations in their published works. However, the illustrated novel (in its traditional sense) has long since passed out of fashion; the emergence of the graphic novel and other illustrated formats is not a replacement. It has been assumed that the traditional novel no longer needs pictures, since pictures are now reader-generated, and there is less confusion about the reader's needs or expectations. I would argue that the proliferation of media sources has helped to define the mainstream novel as a non-visual form.

The essential point is that the history of literature and of writing is, to some extent, studied in schools, but the history of publishing has no place, least of all in the subject called English which, ironically, is entirely reliant on published literary texts for its existence (Goodwyn, 1992). I would argue that the presentation/representation of texts has been principally excluded from the literature domain. One effect of the emergence of Media Education has been to challenge literature teachers to consider textual production and textual construction in new ways. Equally, literature teachers have begun to consider the psychology of readers (rather than just that of the literary author/writer) and to conceptualize the issue of audience in a more powerful way; more of this key point later on.

The computer has enabled any writer, however young, to enter the domain of both the textual designer/typographer and the publisher. Over the last twenty years the term desktop publishing (DTP) has become a reality, especially in the commercial world. Its influence in schools has steadily increased, although it is worth stressing that the majority of writers in school, however talented, will always be, inevitably, immature. Conceptually, I would argue, DTP still belongs to the domain of the publisher; writers in schools need a gradual introduction to the concept of long, detailed texts and they need to move from the mode of passive reader of published text to the active and profoundly different role of *manufacturing* a text. I use the term precisely. They will still, in one sense, be making a manuscript, i.e. a hand/individually created text; a pen was a technology for producing writing, so is a word processor. The extension now is that they have potential control over the whole production process, from the concept of the hand-made text, to the ideal of the exquisitely professional, typographically exact artefact; DTP is therefore a concept that can be introduced in schools and currently made use of by older adolescent writers and, in the future, I think it likely that it will become a feature of the work of much younger writers.

CLOSE READING BECOMES CLOSE WRITING?

A developing practice that illustrates this potential is teachers' recognition of the optimum use of the word processor's 'basic' functions; I think it reasonable now to include colour, certainly on the screen, as a basic.[1] It is simple for an English teacher to select and enter a piece of text into the electronic medium that is 'interesting' in its use of language. Take a poem as a first example, one that has distinctive patterns of rhythm, rhyme and imagery. Students can use the simple functions of bold, italics and colour to interrogate and 'write on' this text. They might first use colour to match rhymes on screen so that all similar rhymes are in the same colour. If the poem has a strong rhythm then students might be able to embolden syllables where they think the stress should be placed. Italics might be used to pick out images such as metaphors and similes. Large type could be used to signal alliteration or even the usually invisible assonance. The resultant text will look, in one way, a chaotic mess; in another way it will be more like a diagram, revealing its own structures and organization. It can be read on screen or printed and compared with the interpretative readings of other students. The teacher has many opportunities to facilitate and monitor discussion around these textual readings.

I would argue that such readings fit closely with reader response theory, and particularly with the pioneering work of Louise Rosenblatt who, long before the word processor existed, has taught us about the way students gradually develop and refine their sense of meaning (Rosenblatt, 1938, 1975). These technologically enhanced screen-readings are tentative responses, first or second readings, enhanced by comparison and contrast with the readings of other students' tentative responses. The most effective medium for these exchanges is talk. However, as Halliday argues, technology has the effect of diminishing 'the gap between spoken and written text' (Halliday, 1996, p. 355). He points out that the tape recorder and the video have turned speech potentially into an object that we can examine and re-examine at leisure and that the computer means that 'writing becomes a happening; it can be scrolled up the screen so that it unfolds in time, like speech' (*ibid.*, p. 355). These 'colouring' techniques are a means of enhancing students' understanding of the ways in which texts employ grammatical means to 'colour' their arguments and so position the reader; they highlight the constructedness of texts which are never neutral conveyors of meaning. This bringing together of speaking and writing is another key convergence that teachers can now begin to turn powerfully to the advantage of all their students.

For example, a piece of prose can be treated more as a section of the linguistic system. Here, students can interrogate text for its grammatical structures. A simple example would involve students analysing a very descriptive passage for its adjectives and adverbs. Colour might be used initially to highlight all words in a certain category, all adjectives in red, all adverbs in blue. Then students might be invited to look at the way such terms are being used, changing font sizes to reflect the degree of emphasis that a reader might place on a word. In complete contrast, students can be given a very plain and deliberately 'dull' text, perhaps one written by an immature writer with a preponderance of 'ands' and 'thens'. Using the 'Find' key they might first count all the repeated conjunctions and connectives and work back through the text replacing these words with a variety of terms that they feel enliven the text and enhance the meaning.

One concept that writers are learning through these activities is that redrafting is an active, developmental process and that one can rewrite existing texts as well as one's own. For many children and adolescents there may be significant value in giving them frequent opportunities to redraft the texts of other writers as a means of making them better rewriters themselves. First, I would argue it is easier to be critical of someone else's text (I use 'critical' in the relatively neutral sense of questioning); with our own texts we often know what we want to say, even if our readers miss our point; with the text of another we often want to ask more of it in order to feel clear about its meaning. Second, it is inevitable that most writers are somewhat defensive about their texts, and we have to learn to see the usefulness of the suggestions of others and to become confident enough to accept some and reject others. Third, all texts are produced through effort; this is a combination of the physical and the mental. At the dramatic end of the spectrum we still produce writer's cramp and finger calluses, we now have repetitive stroke syndrome and the visual fatigue induced by screens. At the more everyday level, every teacher has encountered many children for whom a paragraph is genuinely a massive effort. Put simply then, other texts come to us as gifts; the work, the effort is done. The attraction, even for the reluctant writer, is that the text on the word-processor screen, of whatever quality, is instantly changeable. We could just tinker with it but, as with most human tinkering, we find ourselves drawn in and we start to mess it up to our own satisfaction. The word processor thus draws us in to rewriting in new and innovative ways so that every text contains a potential invitation, not only to a reader, but now to a writer.

PROGRESSIVE WORD PROCESSING?

All English teachers are concerned with helping their students to make progress as writers (and readers) and develop strategies for encouraging writing in a developmental framework. In the next few years the use of technology will demand that we include in this framework the use of the word processor. Whereas currently the computer tends to be for 'finishing off' work, i.e. as an adjunct or extra to 'normal' writing, soon it will be absolutely ordinary and will frequently be the place where writers begin to put down their first 'messy' ideas. It is very likely soon that a total reversal will take place and someone will compose a text, drafting and redrafting it on screen before writing it out by hand, to give it that personal touch. In the next few years, however, we will be finding useful ways to enable students to become progressively better word processors and I offer some ideas here, some from current practice, others more speculative, to consider ways of making optimum use in our teaching of technology to help students learn to write and be better users of technology as writers.

Since the 'Effective Use of Reading' project in the UK in the 1970s (Lunzer and Gardner, 1979) many English teachers have made use of Directed Activities Related to Texts, known as DARTs. The essential aim of this approach was to replace traditional comprehension activities with far more focused and challenging textual activities. Two examples of such activities are cloze procedure and sequencing. Cloze procedure involves removing words from an existing text and asking readers to 'fill in the gaps'. Using a cloze approach on screen is immediately made more interactive by technology as readers/writers can add and delete words in the gaps until they seem 'right'. They can also have access to the 'original' text at the touch of a 'Page down' button if that is helpful. For example, very young writers might read the complete passage first, then work on a version with gaps, perhaps with a list of words to choose from, then compare on screen their version with the original. A sophisticated adolescent writer might be presented with the drafts of a poem and asked to compose a 'final' version. Such a writer might then compose a draft, send and exchange versions with other members of the class before producing his or her final attempt and comparing that on screen with an original. Equally, readers/writers might be provided with a text that has been made bland in some way, for example a piece of scientific writing where the 'difficult' vocabulary has been removed, and asked to 'restore' the text to its proper status. I would argue that this puts students in a demanding and powerful role, and that 'restoring' a text provides an important dimension of writerly responsibility; it requires showing both understanding and respect for a text.

An activity that involves a kind of cloze procedure and develops an understanding of drafting concerns providing students with examples of the various drafts of a poem. In the UK context I have used some of Wilfred Owen's work, especially some if his best-known war poems such as 'Dulce et Decorum Est' and 'Anthem for Doomed Youth'. Some teachers may immediately feel that an objection arises in that the original drafts were pen and paper and that they have a physicality, almost a sacred status, as manuscripts. However, I think that this understanding of the way such manuscripts can be revered can be included within work on this topic. Students can work in a variety of ways. They can begin with the final version of an Owen poem and then work backwards through the drafts; having arrived at the first draft they can then try to write the original using memory and the first draft; this is very definitely a kind of cloze activity.

Alternatively, students can read all the drafts, select the one that they feel has most potential and then revise it or re-present it in what they consider is the most powerful means of enhancing the poem's meaning. Students can create parallel versions on a split screen. This might involve them in placing slightly different versions alongside each other for readers to compare and enjoy, or the final version and one of their own. They might even use the early drafts as clues and deliberately create very different final versions as speculations on where the poem might have gone had certain early ideas been carried through. All such work requires close attention to the original poem and its drafts – it acts therefore as both a linguistic plan and a writing model; the text is a gift to the reader/writer. It is not, however, a blueprint because that implies that there are no gaps to fill, no personal resources to draw on. My contention is that the kind of work outlined above provides a powerful linguistic context within which individual and groups of students can interact with, and influence, a 'great' text. Using these drafts illustrates that poems are worked on and developed over time, and placing them within the electronic medium helps readers/writers to explore their malleability and potential for other meanings, their potential for new and newly 'original' meanings.

Currently students can only have access to the originals via photocopies and as fascimiles via a website. However, they cannot rewrite this form of the original. One has to rewrite them in typed form to provide students with access to an electronic version. I would argue, however, that there is a rich opportunity here for students, not only to examine and work on the various drafts and to see how the final version emerges, but also to consider how our ways of creating texts are changing through electronic media. Wilfred Owen wrote to record his anger and horror at the tragic waste of lives in the First World War; he used the physical means that he had to shape and craft his words into their most effective form. Through technology of various kinds we can now see not only his 'published' work, but also the stages he went through to create that public version. There is also a most important dimension in his attention to the advice of his fellow poet/mentor Siegfried Sassoon. It is possible to trace Sassoon's influence because of the written records that exist. This is a key point. Electronic collaboration usually leaves no trace; there is some loss here in being able to track how the final text was arrived at. This is a helpful point for teachers in reminding students that drafts continue to have value, because they reveal important decisions about writing. Once, when I was extolling the virtues of the word processor to my father, he simply pointed out that I might be losing a good sentence every time I revised it. How would

I know if my earlier ideas were better? This simple point was a valuable corrective to overly naïve enthusiasm. There is considerable scope, therefore, in helping adolescent writers to see that physical texts have a long and intriguing history and that they continue to be a source of new knowledge and ideas.

As well as having access to all these written drafts and records, we now also have access through media technologies to the photographs and film footage of the war, and to more recent reconstructions and representations of film and television makers. Increasingly the Internet provides opportunities for students to search for visual resources of all kinds to use alongside books and other print resources. Students can, through creative use of the photocopier and printer, and increasingly the scanner, produce texts that are a visual representation not only of the poems and their own version, but of the historical and social context from which they came. In that sense, students are 'texting', creating texts that relate to other texts, writing their own texts and designing larger texts that present to the next reader/writer a view of Owen's work, framed by the creator's vision.

Sequencing is another successful DARTs activity which can take on a far more powerful form through electronic means. Currently students are typically presented with a text, usually a poem in 'cut-up' form; the cut-up text might be the fourteen individual lines of a sonnet, or the separated verses of a ballad. The students, often in groups, are asked to sequence these in the best order and to justify their meaning-making. This kind of activity 'works' with students of any age, calling upon their knowledge of words, texts, textual convention and textual coherence strategies. The simplest apparent advantage of electronic sequencing is that no physical, cut-up text is needed, as students simply copy and move on screen as often as they need to. Their version can be presented on screen or printed out if that is important. However, current screens are more limiting than a table; spreading out text and moving it around are helpful and swift ways of rearranging a text. Gathering around a screen can be very focusing, but also, at times, frustrating and limited by the speed of the student at the word processor to cut and paste. What I will now call physical sequencing therefore has some real advantages over what can currently be done on screen and it will retain its importance in the classroom.

Virtual sequencing can occupy a complementary but different place to the physical. With a very short poetic text it can certainly be very effective as an on-screen activity, especially with just a pair of students at work. It can also be very effective when sequencing is linked to cloze, for example, when students might be provided with two-thirds of a complete poem and with the three missing lines to insert, which requires a combination of 'gap' filling and sequencing. However, its potential is considerably greater in the focus it provides on prose or drama.

In studying a play, students might be provided with a section from late on in the text when they have some familiarity with the overall story, a grasp of the main characters and some acquaintance with the language of the dramatist. They might be given the lines from the section in random order and the names of the speaking characters, also some stage directions and then be given the task of sequencing the lines into the 'right' dramatic order. This is a challenging task drawing on dramatic, narrative and linguistic understandings. In some instances teachers might provide scaffolding clues such as 'In this scene Iago tries to provoke Othello's jealousy', or, 'Romeo and Juliet meet for the first time and Shakespeare uses a poetic form to shape their words to each other'. Such work might be accomplished in physical form, but in the electronic form students have far greater finesse in adjusting and positioning lines, and in considering where, and how, the stage directions should be placed.

In the future, this work would be greatly enhanced by the students having electronic access to either still images of actors, or to a video sequence which they could use in parallel with the written text. This facility, rather like an editing suite, would allow them to match lines to facial expressions and possibly movements and actions. A further step would be for them to sequence the text and images and then dub on their own reading of the sequence to test out its dramatic validity. It would be possible for a class to work on different sections of a scene, and then watch them in sequence on their screens to enjoy their 'complete' re-creation.

The opportunities with prose are enormous and I will illustrate this here with some brief examples. One clear benefit comes in understanding the construction of logic and argument. For example, providing students with a piece of argumentative text, randomly re-organized, where the writer has attempted to build up and persuade the reader of a point of view, engages students in a task of identifying and reconstructing the argument. The teacher might go a step further and ask students to create a convincing argument about a specific topic, then supply them with the 'raw material' of an existing writer, again somewhat jumbled, inviting them to use the existing ideas but also to bring in their own and to embellish where they can. Such a task immediately moves students into the world of rhetoric and there is no reason why their sequencing task should not include passages from Plato to Sartre. Richard Lanham (Lanham, 1993) has claimed for many years that one benefit of the 'electronic word' will be to bring the power of rhetoric to a much larger population. He sees this as a profoundly democratic move, bringing new power to the people. This idealistic vision is, in my view, inspirational but unrealizable for some considerable time. However, the inspirational element reminds us that school is the place where democratic ideals and issues can be considered, and where future citizens can be introduced to forms of argument and persuasion that they need to be able to use themselves and, when relevant, to resist or accept from others. Certainly our students in schools will increasingly have access to technology that allows them to undertake these 'texting' activities, and even more so in the world of work and domestic life. It is important for teachers now to have some longer-term views of how such use of the electronic word can be a genuine force for good in the education of all young people. Before taking this argument further forward I need to revisit one key point about computer use which is never merely neutral.

As I indicated in my opening chapter, there are plenty of reasons to be cynical and suspicious about the forms of rhetoric surrounding the notion of 'computer literacy'. I have argued elsewhere (Goodwyn, 1998) that using a computer might be better compared to using a bicycle or a car, making us like cyclists and motorists, simply computerists, i.e. people who know how to use a particular machine. However, teaching is never a simply technical activity; teachers are far more complex than any machine will ever be (Dreyfus and Dreyfus, 1986). One fundamental reason is that teaching is a nurturing and moral activity; good teachers have a respect for pupils' developing independence, but they also challenge prejudices and assumptions. ICT, like motor cars, brings great advantages but also potential problems.

The key point here is that all these ideas about, in a sense, interfering with the texts of others, are aimed at increasing students' understanding of how texts work by getting inside them. Currently students' close reading of a text gives them access to its meanings and structures and they can produce their own text in response. What the electronic text offers is the opportunity to get inside that text and to enhance it or contest it from within. Teachers are thus in a position, practically for the first time, to engage their students with the inner life of a text. This gives great power and scope but also some moral responsibility. This is where teachers need that optimistic vision that keeps them teaching and keeps them believing in the democratic value of education. We should be cynical about some of the claims for 'computer literacy' but we should also be idealistic about the power that students can now have over texts, their own and those of others. Let me now develop this through attention to an especially important piece of language that has taken on key status as a text, Martin Luther King's 'I have a dream' speech.

This is as much the media as the computer age, and it is the convergence of the two that is most significantly changing our concepts of the world. For example, students might study the video of Martin Luther King's 'dream' speech and then a randomly re-organized version of his text. Using the approach to dramatic texts described above, they might then rebuild the speech around a series of stills or the actual video. This initial activity takes them inside the text, the performance of the text and its climactic structure. They might then step outside the text and develop 'contemporary' newspaper or television accounts of the speech and its importance, building in the bias that might be found towards King in different media outlets. This might involve some research into media archives and downloading images and text to be re-presented. The class might also be asked to select the most 'visual' moment from the speech and to create a photo with anchoring caption; they might be asked to place these visual/written texts within an appropriate media text inviting other students to 'guess' the text. Eventually they might be asked to consider the profound importance of texts like 'I have a dream' and be invited to borrow King's model, but not necessarily his biblical language or his particular subject matter, to create their own 'I have a dream' text. Through appropriate use of technology they might create a presentation of their ideals to others. This might involve writing a speech; generating a Powerpoint-style presentation with illustrations and supporting elements of text; or creating a multi-media performance using text, video and audio. King's was a great speech; our students may be no more suited to that rhetorical medium than they are to writing 'great' literary texts. What technology facilitates is the crafting of the powerful expression of their ideals; it gives students access to both presentation and to representation.

Such a task is cognitively and affectively challenging. Asking adolescents to put forward what they believe in and to represent those ideals to others, calls on their inner and outer resources. It also calls upon them to situate who they are in the world, who is this 'I'? Martin Luther King says emphatically, 'I have a dream'. The students are engaged here in deeply personal work, however much they borrow images and texts from the library, the Internet or the television. Technology gifts us, as never before, with the facility to select from cultural resources and to re-present and therefore represent ourselves through them. In my experience our students are already far more comfortable and adept at this than we are; we tend to be the confused and unconfident ones, as Kress argues:

> The old skills are no longer enough; not now, and certainly not in the future. In the face of these changes I do not think we can stay with our old, inherited, contradictory, common sense about communication, representation, meaning-making, in the private and public domain. This is also the world which is utterly normal for my children. None of these things is strange to them. To them what is strange is my puzzlement, dislike, disdain, incomprehension. (Kress, 1997, p. 3)

All artists have confidently absorbed and reused the work of others; I see no mismatch here in comparing T. S. Eliot's 'borrowing' of endless quotations and images from other writers to create *The Waste Land* to this idea of re-assembling existing cultural resources into a work of personal originality. In the media age we need to draw on our visual as well as our linguistic archives. Such work is going on in some schools already, but not many; what I hope this chapter provides is a view of what we can all do now but also of where we are going as the proportion of technologically well-resourced schools steadily increases.

Returning to more current possibilities, another form of challenging sequencing is when texts are deliberately 'mixed up'. It is perhaps best to categorize this activity as 'disentangling'. For example the 'fairy story' below was used in an experiment to test students' understanding of the concept of 'story'; they were invited to consider whether this text 'fitted' the concept or not.

> Once upon a time the beautiful Princess Miranda fell very ill. Her father the King offered half his kingdom to anyone who would cure her. Famous doctors came flocking to the palace with their remedies, but no one could cure the princess. Then there arrived a clever young man, the son of a magician, who said that he could kill the dragon. Next morning

he took his magic sword and after a long battle he cut off the dragon's hideous head. There was much rejoicing in the city. He married the beautiful princess the same day, and they lived happily ever after. (Protherough, 1990, p. 27)

Interestingly, I find that children will not accept this as a story but many adults will. This 'story' is, in fact, two different stories, one a beginning, one an ending. For our purpose here it illustrates the simple point that two 'bits' invite us as readers to make sense of them, especially when the bits come from within a distinct and recognizable genre. Using this text and two or three other examples of 'confused' narrative, students can be asked to 'sort out', to disentangle texts. Some of this work might involve straight sequencing. For example, two short fairy stories might be interwoven into two confused stories and students have to cut and paste the 'bits' until they are two clear stories. Two sequences, one from a scientific text and one from a science fiction novel might be interwoven, or two accounts, one a personal version of an event, one a journalistic account, might be interwoven and students asked to disentangle them. It is just conceivable that such work might be carried out with physical cutting and pasting, but certainly the electronic text makes such work infinitely easier in the way text can be reorganized, and places the emphasis on the intellectual understanding of the students.

CREATING READER-FRIENDLY TEXTS.

Ultimately the finest grained textual details exist in a careful match between the finished text and its rendition, its final representation, typically, in print. The electronic medium allows students, as they move through schooling, to become increasingly sophisticated both as writers and also as textual designers. This latter facility is what makes the word processor such an exciting medium for the future. Student writers can learn about real readers and real audiences; once more we enter the arena of media study. A book is no more a neutral product of technology than a right-wing newspaper or the latest Hollywood film. They not only contain a 'story' version of the world but they are each shaped by the technologies that manufacture them. Most standard word processors now offer what we were calling desktop publishing facilities only a few years ago. The goal of teachers must be, in the twenty-first century, to enable students to comprehend the power this gives them to represent text at its most potent.

Starting with a basic example, using only the typical functions of a word processor, students can revise the reader friendliness of a text; they can begin to experience the act of writing as a design for reading. This design for reading certainly has both psychological and aesthetic dimensions; sometimes these are conflated. I would regard the psychological dimension as the writer's concern for the type of reader who will experience the completed text. For example, it is well-established good practice in many secondary schools for students to write stories for younger readers. This often involves classes in the study of children's books, discussions with young readers and then the drafting and redrafting of a story, perhaps even a 'unique' story for a uniquely real reader. What the writer also needs to consider is how the use of particular fonts and the use of white space will enhance or constrain the reading experience of the young reader. For example, using capitals for complete words or headings makes them much harder to read; more obviously, leaving little space between lines or words inhibits all readers. Centred text is very effective for headings or on posters but tends to be unsuitable for large chunks of text. We identify letters principally by their 'top half' so choosing a fussy font or frequently changing font is very uncomfortable for young (and old) readers. These aspects of textual design can now be taught to students; they can easily try them out on screen or in draft format before producing a definitive representation. For the vast majority of students this attention to both the psychology of textual design and its aesthetic satisfactions was never possible before. Writers can become powerfully self-conscious readers.

It is hard to say at what point humanity became aware that its written systems were not just versions of its speech systems, or at exactly what point something called 'Linguistics' discovered that language does not just name and represent a physical universe. We have always been quintessentially living through symbols; this was never more powerfully apparent than now.

One important element in looking at our students' needs in the future is inevitably our concern for how they will live, both how they will 'make a living' and how they will 'live a full' life. Reich puts forward a view of future work as occupying three categories: 'routine production services, in-person services and symbolic-analytic services' (Reich, 1992, p. 177). His argument is that the last category will be by far the most valuable and valued. Whether readers accept these rather tidy categories or not is another matter and I do not suggest that schools should be simply responding to the 'needs of industry/utilitarian argument'. What I think most likely is that they will accept that more and more of their future students will spend a significant amount of their time focused on a screen. This screen may be filled with numerical symbols or linguistic symbols in relation to work, or it might equally be filled with real pictures of today's news or fantasy figures from the latest virtual reality game. I use the term 'significant' more to suggest important, than merely copious, in terms of time. We are increasingly aware of the ergonomic factors relating to repetitive use of computers in particular, and should become better at managing our time; people who read books all day know that there is a cost to their bodies and especially their eyes in such unbalanced concentration. The important point is that the interaction with the screen and its symbolic contents will be highly significant in terms of its material value and its status.

Some readers might react to this idea with the simple point that what most students need is more time with books, more time with basic reading and writing than with the screen, whether computer, televisual or cinematic. In my view these activities are not 'either/or' nor are they oppositional. The task for schools is to recognize that our students do need to become symbolic analysts. Being a symbolic analyst sounds very different to being a literate citizen but,

I would argue, when by literate we mean highly literate then being a symbolic analyst is an exact description of that individual's capabilities. Literate citizens can understand and manipulate symbols to their advantage. The greatest danger with the stress on 'basics' is that they hold us back from accepting the 'complexics' of symbolic analysis. Because symbols are attempts at representation they are at once exact and multi-meaningful; that is, we can interpret them exactly for our interpretative purpose but, at the same time, recognize their potential for other meanings.

What does this point have to do with students and texts? Texts are attempts at meaningful representation; since they are produced through a choice from a range of options they inevitably generate many meanings. Technology allows students to get inside texts in ways that are still new, but will soon be familiar. They are becoming textists, writers/readers who can manipulate every dimension of a text, from its ultimate overall shape and appearance to the repositioning of a single punctuation mark. This power allows for the creation of more meanings, sometimes perhaps more exact, more precise, in other contexts more ambiguous, more mysteriously symbolic.

Small children in all cultures begin their consciousness of life through trying to represent the world symbolically, through trying out language and play. Education systems do try to build on this, although they also bring in a vital awareness of the symbolic efforts of others, hence English teachers want students to read the good poems of others and write good poems of their own. As the technologies of the media and the computer converge, so the extent of the symbolic resources available to us dramatically increases. English teachers are well placed to enable their students not just to produce texts that read well and look good, but that aspire to the level of the representational, the attempt to maximize meaning.

CONCLUSION

As this chapter, and this whole collection, illustrates, there is much inspirational and exciting work already going on in many schools, but we are also now able to recognize just how far that work might take all teachers and their students. We will retain our critical edge and teachers will never accept technology without question; there are plenty of points of caution expressed throughout this book. However, as I have tried to show, we have not even begun to make real use of the existing textual power of the word processor. As our ability to bring all kinds of textual and visual resources together rapidly develops through convergent media and computer technologies, we do enter a new age of enormous creative scope.

NOTE

1. This practice is now being used by a number of people but I should like to express my acknowledgement to Chris Warren who certainly was the first person to help me see just how far we had underused these 'basic' functions.

Bibliography

Chapter 1
Cox, B. (1991) *Cox on Cox*. London: Hodder and Stoughton.
DES (1989) *English from Ages 5–16*. London: HMSO.
Goodson, I. F. and Mangan, J. M. (1996) 'Computer literacy as ideology', *British Journal of Sociology of Education*, Vol. 17, No. 1, pp. 65–79.
Goodwyn, A. (1992) *English Teaching and Media Education*. Buckingham: Open University Press.
Goodwyn, A. (1997a) *Developing English Teachers*. Buckingham: Open University Press.
Goodwyn, A. (1997b) *Interim Evaluation of the Information Technology in English Project*. London: DfEE.
Goodwyn, A. (1998) *Final Evaluation of the Information Technology in English Project*. London: DfEE.
Goodwyn, A. (ed.) (1998) *Literary and Media Texts in Secondary English*. London: Cassell.
Goodwyn, A., Adams, A. and Clarke, S. (1997) 'The future of literacy', *The Journal of Information Technology in Teacher Education*, Vol. 6, No. 3, pp. 227–39.
Goodwyn, A. and Findlay, K. (1999) 'The Cox models revisited: English Teachers' views of their subject and of the National Curriculum', *English in Education*, Vol. 33, No. 2, Summer, NATE Sheffield, pp. 19–31.
Kress, G. (1997) *Before Writing: Rethinking the Paths to Literacy*. London: Routledge.
Moore, P. (1986) *Using Computers in English: A Practical Guide*. London: Routledge.
Richards, I. A. (1924) *Principles of Literary Criticism*. London: Routledge and Kegan Paul.
Tweddle, S., Adams, A., Clarke, S., Scrimshaw, P. and Walton, S. (1997) *English for Tomorrow*. Buckingham: Open University Press.
Warren, H. and Page, F. (eds) (1953) *Tennyson: Complete Poems and Plays*. Oxford: Oxford University Press.

Chapter 2
Actis (1997) *Review of Software for Use in English*, available from Actis Ltd, Lakeside Business Centre, The Field, Shipley Country Park, Derbyshire DE75 7JQ; tel. 01773 534000 or from Chris.Warren@actis.co.uk.
Andrews, R. (1996) 'Visual literacy in question', *20:20*, No. 4, June 1996, pp. 17–20.
Andrews, R. (ed.) (1997) *English in Education*, Vol. 31, No. 2 (special edition on Electronic English).

Andrews, R. and Clarke, S. (1996) 'Information technology, information and the English curriculum', *The English and Media Magazine*, 35, November, pp. 35–9.

Andrews, R. and Reid, M. (1998) Unpublished notes on the future of ICT in English. Hinckley: BECTa conference on ICT in subject teaching, December 1988.

Andrews, R. and Simons, M. (1996) 'The electronic word: multimedia, rhetoric and English teaching', *The English and Media Magazine*, 35, November, pp. 40–3.

British Film Institute/Channel 4 (1997) *Backtracks: Interact with Sound and Vision.* London: BFI.

English and Media Centre (1997) *Picture Power: The CD-Rom*, available from The English and Media Centre, Chalton Street, London NW1 1RX; tel. 0171 383 0488, e-mail: engmedcentre@bbcnc.org.uk or englishandmedia@dial.pipex.com.

Goodwyn, A. and Findlay, K. (1999) 'The Cox Models revisited: English teachers' views of their subject and of the National Curriculum', *English in Education*, Vol. 33, No. 2, Summer, pp. 19–31.

Graves, D. (1982) *Writing: Teachers and Children at Work.* Portsmouth NH: Heinemann.

Harrison, C. (1997) Unpublished evaluation of Multimedia Portables in Schools pilot. Nottingham: School of Education.

Kress, G. (1997) *Before Writing: Rethinking the Paths to Literacy.* London: Routledge.

Lanham, R. (1993) *The Electronic Word: Democracy, Technology and the Arts.* Chicago: University of Chicago Press.

Morgan, W. and Andrews, R. (1999) 'City of text? Metaphors for hypertext in literary education', *Changing English*, 6.1, March 1999.

NCET (1997a) *IT in English Materials.* Coventry: NCET.

NCET (1997b) *A Review of Software for Curriculum Use.* Coventry: NCET.

Photographers' Gallery (1997) *Rosendale Odyssey*, website hosted by ARTEC at http://www.artec.org.uk/rosendale/.

Raney, K. (1997) *Visual Literacy: Current Debates.* London: Middlesex University School of Education.

Raney, K. (in press) *Show and Tell: Conversations about Visual Literacy.* London: Middlesex University Press (Research in Education series).

Smith, F. (1980) *Writing.* Portsmouth NH: Heinemann.

Stannard, R. (1997) 'Navigating cyberspace: vision, textuality and the World Wide Web', *English in Education*, Vol. 31, No. 2, Summer, NATE Sheffield, pp. 14–22.

Tweddle, S. (1997) 'A retrospective: fifteen years of computers in English', *English in Education*, Vol. 31, No. 2, pp. 5–13.

Twentieth Century Fox Film Corporation (1998) *Great Expectations*, interactive educational CD-Rom (with Film Education and Foresight New Media). See also website at http://www.greatexpectations.co.uk.

Chapter 3

DENI (1997) *A Strategy for Education Technology in Northern Ireland.* Belfast: DENI.

Goodwyn, A., Adams, A. and Clarke, S. (1997) 'The great god of the future: the views of current and future English teachers on the place of IT in literacy', *English in Education*, Vol. 31, No. 2, pp. 54–62.

Chapter 4

Bereiter, C. and Scardamalia, M. (1987) *The Psychology of Written Composition.* Hillsdale, NJ: Lawrence Erlbaum Associates.

Bigum, C. and Green, B. (1992) 'Technologizing literacy: the dark side of the dream', *Australian Journal of Education*, Vol. 12, No. 2, pp. 4–28.

Burbules, N. (1997a) 'Rhetorics of the web: hyperreading and critical literacy'. In Snyder, I. (ed.) *Page to Screen: Taking Literacy into the Electronic Era.* St Leonards, NSW: Allen and Unwin.

Burbules, N. (1997b) 'Misinformation, malinformation, messed-up information, and mostly useless information: how to avoid getting tangled up in the 'Net'. In Lankshear, C. *et al.* (1997) *Digital Rhetorics: Literacies and Technologies in Education – Current Practices and Future Directions*, Vol. 3. Canberra: Department of Employment, Education, Training and Youth Affairs.

Cumming, J., Wyatt-Smith, C., Ryan, J. and Doig, S. (1998) *The Literacy-Curriculum Interface: The Literacy Demands of the Curriculum in Post-compulsory Schooling.* Canberra: DEETYA.

Graham, J. and Martin, R. (1998) 'Teachers, schools and the new technologies: a discussion paper', *Australian Educational Computing*, Vol. 13, No. 2, pp. 6–12.

Hofer, B. and Pintrich, P. (1997) 'The development of epistemological theories: Beliefs about knowledge and knowing and their relation to learning', *Review of Educational Research*, Vol. 67, No. 1, pp. 88–140.

Johnson-Eilola (1997) 'Living on the surface, learning in the age of global communication networks'. In Snyder, I. (ed.) *Page to Screen: Taking Literacy into the Electronic Era.* St Leonards, NSW: Allen and Unwin.

Jordan, K. (1999) 'Can anybody get the ball rolling: the role of a student moderator', *English in Australia*, No. 124, April.

Kress, G. (1997) 'Visual and verbal modes of representation in electronically mediated communication: the potentials of new forms of texts'. In Snyder, I. (ed.) *Page to Screen: Taking Literacy into the Electronic Era.* St Leonards, NSW: Allen and Unwin.

Langer, J. and Applebee, A. (1987). 'How writing shapes thinking: a study of teaching and learning', *NCTE Research Rep. No. 22.* National Council of Teachers of English.

Lankshear, C., Bigum, C., Durrant, C., Green, B., Honan, E., Morgan, W., Murray, J., Snyder, and Wild, M. (1997) *Digital Rhetorics: Literacies and Technologies in Education – Current Practices and Future Directions*, Vols 1–3. Canberra: DEETYA.

Lankshear, C., Gee, J., Knobel, M. and Searle, C. (1997) *Changing Literacies.* Buckingham: Open University Press.

Morgan, W. (1997) *Critical Literacy in the Classroom: The Art of the Possible.* London and New York: Routledge.

Prain, V. (1998) *Naming Futures for Critical Literacy English in Australia,* 122, pp. 122–7.

Sefton-Green, J. (ed.) (1998) *Digital Diversions: Youth Culture in the Age of Multimedia.* London: University College London Press.

Smith and Curtin (1997) 'Children, computer and life online: education in a cyber world'. In Snyder, I. (ed.) *Page to Screen: Taking Literacy into the Electronic Era.* St Leonards, NSW: Allen and Unwin.

Snyder, I. (ed.) (1997) *Page to Screen: Taking Literacy into the Electronic Era.* St Leonards, NSW: Allen and Unwin.

TeachersOnLine@www.actf.com.au/tol/.

Chapter 5

Cotton, B. and Oliver, R. (1992) *Understanding Hypermedia.* London: Phaidon, p. 88.

Crystal, D. (1998) 'Interpreting interlanguage', *The A Level English Magazine*, No. 1, September.

Johnston, C. (1998) 'Battleground moves to the home front', *TES Online Computers in Education*, 20 November.

Kress, G. (1995) *Writing the Future – English and the Making of a Culture of Innovation.* Sheffield: NATE, pp. 3 and 23.

Montgomery, M., Fabb, N., Furniss, T., Mills, S. and Durant, A. (1992) *Ways of Reading.* London: Routledge, p. 192.

Turkle, S. (1996) *Life on the Screen – Identity in the Age of the Internet.* London: Wiedenfeld and Nicholson, p. 30.

Chapter 6

Barthes, R. (1974) *S/Z*. Translated by Richard Miller. New York: Hill & Wang.

Bazalgette, C. (1992) 'Key aspects of media education'. In Alvarado, M. and Boyd-Barrett, O. (eds) *Media Education: An Introduction*. London: BFI Publishing, pp. 199–219.

Beach, R. (1993) *A Teacher's Introduction to Reader-response Theories*. Urbana, IL: National Council of Teachers of English.

Bigelow, B. (1995) 'On the road to cultural bias: A critique of the *Oregon Trail* CD-Rom', *Rethinking Schools*, Vol. 10, No. 1, pp. 14–18.

Buckingham, D. and Sefton-Green, J. (1994) *Cultural Studies Goes to School: Reading and Teaching Popular Media*. London: Taylor & Francis.

Carnes, M. (ed.) (1996) *Past Imperfect: History According to the Movies*. New York: Owl Books.

Crotty, C. (1998) '*Macworld*'s hall of fame presents 20 unforgettable games'. *Macworld*, December, p. 73, review of the CD-Rom's *Myst* and *Riven*.

Cyan (Producer) (1998) *The Making of Riven*. Novato, CA: Cyan, Inc., film on CD-Rom.

Keith, W. H. and Barton, N. (1997) *Official Riven: The Sequel to Myst Player's Guide*. www.bradygames.com: Brady Games.

Langer, J. A. (ed.) (1992) *Literature Instruction: A Focus on Student Response*. Urbana, Illinois: NCTE.

MECC (1997) *Oregon Trail II. School Version*. Minneapolis, MN: The Learning Company, Inc., CD-Rom.

Miller, R., Miller, R. (Designers) and Strand, L. (Producer) (1993) *Myst*. Novato, CA: Cyan, Inc.

Miller, R. and Miller, R. with Wingrove, D. (1995) *Myst: Book of Atrus*. New York: Hyperion.

Miller, R., Van der Wende, R. (Designer and Director) and Miller, R. (Producer) (1997) *Riven: The Sequel to Myst*. Novato, CA: Cyan, Inc., CD-Rom.

Murray, J. H. (1997) *Hamlet on the Holodeck: The Future of Narrative in Cyberspace*. Cambridge, MA: MIT Press.

Rosenblatt, L. M. (1978) *The Reader, the Text, the Poem: The Transactional Theory of the Literary Work*. Carbondale, IL: Southern Illinois University Press.

Sanger, J. with Wilson, J., Davies, B. and Whitakker, R. (1997) *Young Children, Videos, and Computer Games: Issues for Teachers and Parents*. London: Falmer Press.

Scholes, R. (1985) *Textual Power: Literary Theory and the Teaching of English*. New Haven, CT: Yale University Press.

Wolf, D. P. (1988) *Reading Reconsidered*. New York: College Entrance Examination Board.

Chapter 7

Clarke, S. (1995) 'Is "N.C." English never changing? Shakespeare and the new information technologies', *English in Education*, Vol. 29, No. 2, pp. 12–19.

Davies, A. and Wells, S. (1994) *Shakespeare and the Moving Image*. Cambridge: Cambridge University Press.

DES (1990) *English in the National Curriculum*. London: HMSO.

DFE (1995) *DFE English for Ages 5–16*. London: HMSO.

DfEE (1998) *Circular 4/98 Teaching: High Status, High Standards*. London: DfEE.

Dixon, J. (1991) *A Schooling in English: Critical Episodes in the Struggle to Shape Literary and Cultural Studies*. Buckingham: Open University Press.

Donaldson, P. (1997) 'Digital archive as expanded text: Shakespeare and electronic textuality'. In Sutherland, K. (ed.) *Electronic Text*. Oxford: Clarendon Press.

Friedlander, L. (1991) 'The Shakespeare project'. In Delaney, P. and Landow, G. (eds) *Hypermedia and Literary Studies*. Cambridge, Massachusetts: MIT Press.

Hewins, A. (ed.) (1981) *The Dillen; Memories of a Man of Stratford Upon Avon*.

Oxford: Oxford University Press.

Lanham, R. (1993) *The Electronic Word: Democracy, Technology and the Arts*. Chicago: University of Chicago Press.

Reynolds, P. (1991) 'Unlocking the box: Shakespeare on film and video'. In Aers, L. and Wheale, N. (eds) *Shakespeare in the Changing Curriculum*. London: Routledge.

Shayer, D. (1972) *Teaching English 1900–1970*. London: Routledge and Kegan Paul.

Sutherland, K. (1997) 'Introduction'. In Sutherland, K. (ed.) *Electronic Text*. Oxford: Clarendon Press.

Chapter 8

DFE (1995) *English for Ages 5–16*. London: HMSO.

Dreyfus, H. L. and Dreyfus, S. E. (1986) *Mind Over Machine: The Power of Human Intuition and Expertise in the Computer Era*. Oxford: Basil Blackwell.

Goodwyn, A. (1992) *English Teaching and Media Education*. Buckingham: Open University Press.

Goodwyn, A. (1997) *Information Technology in English Project: Interim Evaluation*. London: DES.

Goodwyn, A. (ed.) (1998) *Literary and Media Texts in Secondary English*. London: Cassell.

Halliday, M. A. K. (1996) 'Literacy and linguistics: a functional perspective'. In Hasan, R. and Williams, G. (eds) *Literacy and Society*. London: Longman.

Kress, G. (1997) *Before Writing: Rethinking the Paths to Literacy*. London: Routledge.

Lanham, R. (1993) *The Electronic Word: Democracy, Technology and the Arts*. Chicago: The University of Chicago Press.

Lunzer, E. and Gardner, K. (1979) *The Effective Use of Reading*. London: Heinemann.

Protherough, R. (1990) 'Children's recognition of stories'. In Hayhoe, M. and Parker, S. (eds) *Reading and Response*. Buckingham: Open University Press.

Reich, R. (1992) *The Work of Nations*. New York: Vintage.

Rosenblatt, L. (1938) *Literature as Exploration*. New York: Modern Language Association.

Rosenblatt, L. (1975) *The Reader, The Text, The Poem: The Transactional Theory of the Literary Work*. Carbondale, IL: Southern Illinois University Press.

Smith, F. (1982) *Writing and the Writer*. London: Heinemann.

Index